ADVEN

Pembrokeshire
Coast Path

■ This new publication covers the Pembrokeshire Coast Path, a National Trail extending 174 miles from St. Dogmaels to Amroth, traversing the varied coastline of the Pembrokeshire National Park.

■ Containing Ordnance Survey 'Explorer' maps in a convenient book format with an index to the main features, and showing all footpaths, rights of way and public access land, this is the essential companion whether tackling the entire route or enjoying a relaxing afternoon walk.

CONTENTS

Reference / Legend.................2-3
Key to Map Pages...................4-5
Map Pages...........................6-79
Index.................................. 80-85

Route Planner......................86-87
Safety & Security......................88
QR codes................................89

A-Z AZ AtoZ
— registered trade marks of —
Geographers' A-Z Map Company Ltd

www. / az.co.uk

EDITION 1 2014
Copyright © Geographers' A-Z Map Company Ltd.
Telephone: 01732 781000 (Enquiries & Trade Sales)
01732 783422 (Retail Sales)
© Crown copyright and database rights 2014. Ordnance Survey 100017302.
1:25 000 'Explorer' maps are sourced from Ordnance Survey.
Public rights of way shown on these maps have been taken from local authority definitive maps and later amendments.
The representation on the maps of any other road, track or footpath is no evidence of the existence of a right of way.
© Natural England (2014) material is reproduced with the permission of Natural England, http://www.naturalengland.org.uk/copyright

Communications

ROADS AND PATHS
Not necessarily rights of way

  Service Areas   Junction number

M I or A 6(M) — Motorway

A 35 — Dual carriageway

A 30 — Main road

B 3074 — Secondary road

Narrow road with passing places

Road under construction

Road generally more than 4m wide

Road generally less than 4m wide

Other road, drive or track, fenced and unfenced

Gradient: steeper than 20% (1 in 5); 14% (1 in 7) to 20% (1 in 5)

 Ferry; Ferry P – passenger only

Path

RAILWAYS

Multiple track standard gauge

Single track standard gauge

Narrow gauge or Light rapid transit system (LRTS) and station

Road over; road under; level crossing

Cutting; tunnel; embankment

Station, open to passengers; siding

PUBLIC RIGHTS OF WAY

----------- Footpath   — — — — — Bridleway

+ + + + + + Byway open to all traffic

-+-+-+-+- Restricted byway (not for use by mechanically propelled vehicles)

Public rights of way shown on this map have been taken from local authority definitive maps and later amendments. Rights of way are liable to change and may not be clearly defined on the ground.
Please check with the relevant local authority for the latest information.

The representation on this map of any other road, track or path is no evidence of the existence of a right of way.

OTHER PUBLIC ACCESS

• • • Other routes with public access (not normally shown in urban areas)

The exact nature of the rights on these routes and the existence of any restrictions may be checked with the local highway authority. Alignments are based on the best information available.

 National Trail

Pembrokeshire Coast Path

Long Distance Route and Recreational Route

------------ Permissive footpath

— — — — Permissive bridleway

Footpaths and bridleways along which landowners have permitted public use but which are not rights of way. The agreement may be withdrawn.

• • • Traffic-free cycle route

 National cycle network route number – traffic free

 National cycle network route number – on road

 DANGER AREA   Firing and test ranges in the area. Danger! Observe warning notices

Visit www.access.mod.uk

ACCESS LAND

Portrayal of access land on this map is intended as a guide to land which is normally available for access on foot, for example access land created under the Countryside and Rights of Way Act 2000, and land managed by the National Trust, Forestry Commission and Woodland Trust. Access for other activities may also exist. Some restrictions will apply; some land will be excluded from open access rights.
The depiction of rights of access does not imply or express any warranty as to its accuracy or completeness. Observe local signs and follow the Countryside Code.

Visit www.ccw.gov.uk for up-to-date information

Access land boundary and tint

Access land in woodland area

 Access information point

 MANAGED ACCESS   Access permitted within managed controls for example, local bylaws

Visit www.access.mod.uk

General Information

BOUNDARIES

— + — + — National

— · — · — County (England)

—— —— Unitary Authority (UA), Metropolitan District (Met Dist), London Borough (LB) or District (Scotland & Wales are solely Unitary Authorities)

· · · · · · · · · · Civil Parish (CP) (England) or Community (C) (Wales)

—— —— National Park boundary

VEGETATION

Limits of vegetation are defined by positioning of symbols

Coniferous trees

Non-coniferous trees

Coppice

Bracken, heath or rough grassland   Orchard

Marsh, reeds or saltings   Scrub

GENERAL FEATURES

+	Place of worship	△	Triangulation pillar; mast	BP/BS	Boundary post/stone
	Current or former place of worship	✗	Windmill, with or without sails	CG	Cattle grid
	with tower		Wind pump; wind turbine	CH	Clubhouse
	with spire, minaret or dome			FB	Footbridge
□ ▭	Building; important building	pylon pole	Electricity transmission line	MP ; MS	Milepost; milestone
▨	Glasshouse	ⅲⅲ	Slopes	Mon	Monument
▲	Youth hostel			PO	Post office
■	Bunkhouse/camping barn/other hostel	Gravel pit — Sand pit		Pol Sta	Police station
⛟	Bus or coach station			Sch	School
Lighthouse; disused lighthouse; beacon		Other pit or quarry — Landfill site or slag/spoil heap		TH	Town hall
				NTL	Normal tidal limit
				W; Spr	Well; spring

HEIGHTS AND NATURAL FEATURES

52 · Ground survey height

284 · Air survey height

Surface heights are to the nearest metre above mean sea level. Where two heights are shown, the first height is to the base of the triangulation pillar and the second (in brackets) to the highest natural point of the hill.

Vertical face/cliff

75
60
50

Contours may be at 5 or 10 metres vertical interval

Loose rock   Boulders   Outcrop   Scree

Water

Mud

Sand; sand & shingle

ARCHAEOLOGICAL AND HISTORICAL INFORMATION

⚔	Site of antiquity	* ⅲⅲ	Visible earthwork	Information provided by English Heritage for England and the Royal Commissions on the Ancient and Historical Monuments for Scotland and Wales
⚔ 1066	Site of battle (with date)	VILLA	Roman	
		Castle	Non-Roman	

Selected Tourist and Leisure Information

P	Parking	X	Camp site	🚲	Cycle hire		Fishing
P&R	Park & Ride, - all year		Caravan site	U	Horse riding	☆	Other tourist feature
P&R	- seasonal	Ⓧ	Recreation leisure sports centre	☀	Viewpoint	✝	Cathedral/Abbey
𝒊	Information cen. - all year	⚑	Golf course or links	X	Picnic site	🏛	Museum
𝒊	- seasonal		Theme pleasure park	ⅷ	Country park		Castle/fort
V	Visitor centre	🚂	Preserved railway	❁	Garden arboretum		Building of historic interest
	Forestry Commission visitor centre	🍺	Public house/s	⛵	Water activities	HC	Heritage centre
PC	Public convenience	⚒	Craft centre	✈	Slipway		National Trust
✆	Telephone - public	❗	Walks/trails	⛵	Boat trips		Cadw (Welsh Heritage)
✆	- roadside assistance	🚲	Cycle trail	⚓	Boat hire	◈	World Heritage site/area
✆	- emergency		Mountain bike trail	🦆	Nature reserve		

1 Kilometre = 0.6214 mile
1 metre = 3.2808 feet

Scale 1:25 000

1 mile = 1.6093 kilometres
100 feet = 30.48 metres

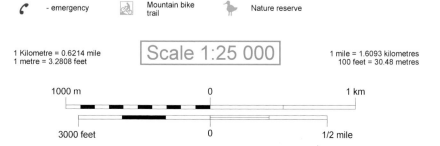

1000 m   0   1 km

3000 feet   0   1/2 mile

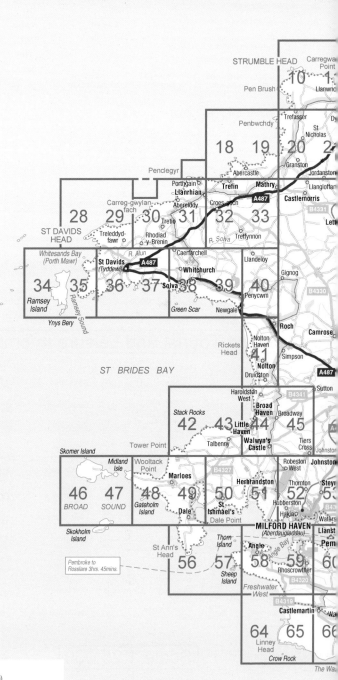

STRUMBLE HEAD | Carregwa Point

10 | 1

Pen Brush | Llanwnc

Trefasser | St Nicholas

Penbwchdy | Dy

18 | 19 | 20 | 2

Abercastle | Granston | Jordanston

Penclegyr | Porthgain | Trefin | Mathry | Castlemorris

Llanrhian | Croes-goch | A487 | B4331 | Let

Carreg-gwylan-fach | Abereiddy | Tretio

28 | 29 | 30 | 31 | 32 | 33

ST DAVIDS HEAD | Treleddyd-fawr | Rhodiad-y-Brenin | Treffynnon

R. Alun | Caerfarchell | Llandeloy

Whitesands Bay (Porth Mawr) | St Davids (Tyddewi) | A487 | Whitchurch | Gignog

34 | 35 | 36 | 37 | 38 | 39 | 40 | B4330

Ramsey Island | Solva | Penycwm

Ynys Bery | Ramsey Sound | Green Scar | Newgale | Roch | Camrose

Rickets Head | Nolton Haven | Simpson

ST BRIDES BAY | 41 | A487

Nolton | Druidston | Sutton

Haroldston West | B4341

Broad Haven | Broadway

Stack Rocks | 42 | 43 | 44 | 45

Little Haven | Tiers Cross

Tower Point | Talbenny | Walwyn's Castle | Johnsto

Skomer Island | Midland Isle | Wooltack Point | Roberston West | Johnston

Grassholm Island | Marloes | B4327 | Thornton | 52 | Steyn

Herbrandston | 51 | B43

46 | 47 | 48 | 49 | 50 | Hubberston | Waters

BROAD | SOUND | Gateholm Island | Dale | St Ishmael's | Hakin

Skokholm Island | Dale Point | MILFORD HAVEN (Aberdaugleddau) | Lianst

St Ann's Head | Thorn Island | Angle | 59 | Pem

Pembroke to Rosslare 3hrs. 45mins. | 56 | 57 | 58 | Rhoscrowther | 60

Sheep Island | Freshwater West | B4320

Castlemartin | B4319

64 | 65 | 66

Linney Head | Crow Rock | The Wa

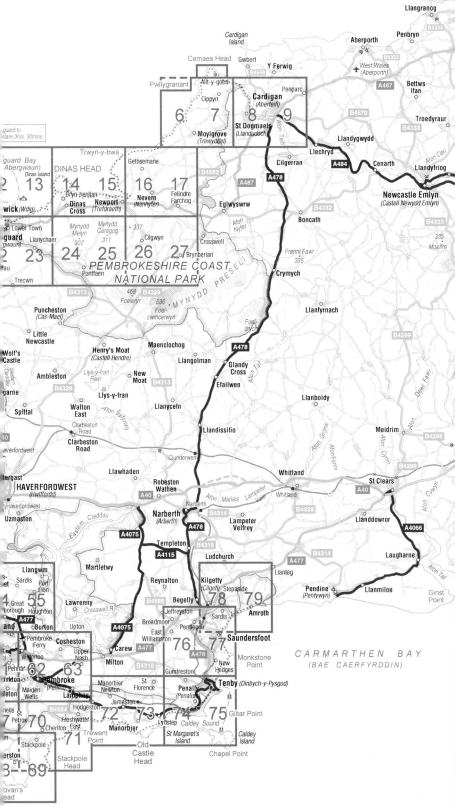

Llangranog

Aberporth

Penbryn

B4334

Bettws
Ifan

West Wales
(Aberporth)

A487

Cardigan
Island

Cemaes Head

Gwbert

Y Ferwig

Troedyraur

B4333

Pwllygranant

Allt-y-goed

Penparc

Cardigan
(Aberteifi)

B4570

Llandygwydd

Cippyn

St Dogmaels
(Llandudoch)

Afon Teifi

Llechryd

A484

Cenarth

Llandyfriog

guard to
clare 3hrs. 30mins.

Moylgrove
(Trewyddel)

Cilgerran

A478

Newcastle Emlyn
(Castell Newydd Emlyn)

6

7

8

9

B4333

guard Bay
Abergwaun)

Dinas Island

13

DINAS HEAD

Trwyn-y-bwa

Gethsemane

A4582

B4332

Boncath

335
Moelfre

14

15

16

17

A487

Bryn-henllan

Dinas
Cross

Newport
(Trefdraeth)

Nevern
(Nanhyfer)

Felindre
Farchog

Eglwyswrw

wick (Wdig)

Lower Town

guard
gwaun)

Llanychaer

23

24

25

26

27

Mynydd
Melyn
307

Mynydd
Caregog
311

337

Cilgwyn

Crosswell

Brynberian

Afon
Nyfer

Crymych

Trecwn

PEMBROKESHIRE COAST
NATIONAL PARK

Pontfaen

B4313

468
Foeleryr

A4329

536
Foel-
cwmcerwyn

MYNYDD PRESELI

Frenni Fawr
395

Puncheston
(Cas-Mael)

Llanfyrnach

B4299

Little
Newcastle

Wolf's
Castle

Maenclochog

Foel
drych

A478

Henry's Moat
(Castell Hendre)

Llangolman

Llanboidy

Meidrim

B4298

Ambleston

garne

Llys-y-fran
Resr.

New
Moat

Glandy
Cross

B4313

B4329

Llys-y-fran

Llanycefn

Efailwen

Afon Taf

B4299

Spittal

Walton
East

Afon Syfynwy

Clarbeston
Road

10

averfordwest

Clarbeston
Road

Llandissilio

St Clears

A40

Llanddowror

Clunderwen

Afon Cynin

A40

Whitland

A4066

Llawhaden

Whitland

Laugharne

HAVERFORDWEST
(Hwlffordd)

Robeston
Wathen

Afon Marlais

Lampeter
Vale

B4328

B4314

Afon Taf

Haverfordwest

Eastern Cleddau

A40

Narberth

Narberth
(Arberth)

A478

B4314

Lampeter
Velfrey

A477

Uzmaston

ergast

A4075

Templeton

B4315

Ludchurch

Llanteg

Pendine
(Pentywyn)

Llanmiloe

Ginst
Point

and

A4115

Reynalton

Kilgetty
(Cilgetti)

Stepaside

Langwm

Sardis

Port
Lion

Martletwy

Begelly

78

79

Great
borough

Houghton

55

Lawrenny

Cresswell R.

Jeffreyston

Amroth

A477

Burton

Upton

Broadmoor

Pentlepoir

Sardis

Saundersfoot

CARMARTHEN BAY
(BAE CAERFYRDDIN)

Pembroke
Ferry

Coshaston

Carew

East
Williamston

76

77

Monkstone
Point

Waterloo

Upper
Nash

A477

Milton

B4318

Gumfreston

New
Hedges

Pennar

62

63

Pembroke
(Penfro)

Lamphey

Manorbier
Newton

St
Florence

Penally
(Penalun)

Tenby (Dinbych-y-Pysgod)

onkton
leton

Maiden
Wells

B4584

Jameston

Hodgeston

72

73

74

75

Gitar Point

70

Cheriton

Freshwater
East

Manorbier

Lydstep

Caldey Sound

Caldey
Island

St
Petrox

71

Trewent
Point

Old
Castle
Head

St Margaret's
Island

Chapel Point

69

Stackpole
Head

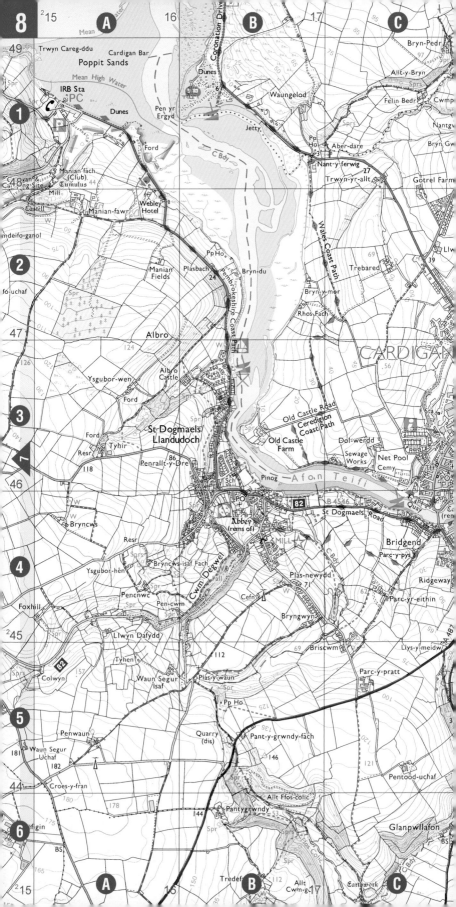

1

43

2

42

3

41

Cafnau
Pen Sidan
Aber Pensidan

14

Aber Careg-y-Fran
Pen Sidan
Careg-y-Fran

4

Pen
Ca 40

Pwll
Cwn

Pwll Gwylog

Cwm Gwy

5

Fishguard Bay/
Bae Abergwaun

Cerrig Duon

39

Penrhyn   Carreg
Erw-goch   Pen-las

Aber Bach

Aber
Hywel

Penrhyn
Mawr

Penrhyn
Ychen   Ford

Pwll y   Aber   Hes-cwm-
Blewyn   Grugog   isaf

6

Pont
y Meddyg

Aber   Trewrach
Richard

Penrhyn   FB

Pen

Y Das

Needle
Rock   38

Cave

18 82 Ⓐ 83 Ⓑ 84 Ⓒ

38

❶

37

❷

36

❸

²35

❹

34

Ynys Deullyn

Caves

Pen Castell-coch   Castell Coch   Cwn
                                                  Bada

Pwll Whiting   Caves   Wales Coast Path

❺   Longhouse   Sa

Pwll Llong
Waterfall

FB

Pwll Olfa

33

Trwyn Llwyd

Trwyn
Elen

Ynys-fach
Caves   Pits
                         (dis)

❻ Llanlleifer   Trefin/
Pembrokeshire Coast Path Aber Draw   Trevine
              Pwll Crochan Clychau
              Waterfall   Waterfall
thgain   Caves   FB   POR   63
        Pit   Spr
        (dis) Ⓐ   32   Ⓑ   84   Ⓒ
82   83 yn-y-Dor   ommins
                                            Mawr

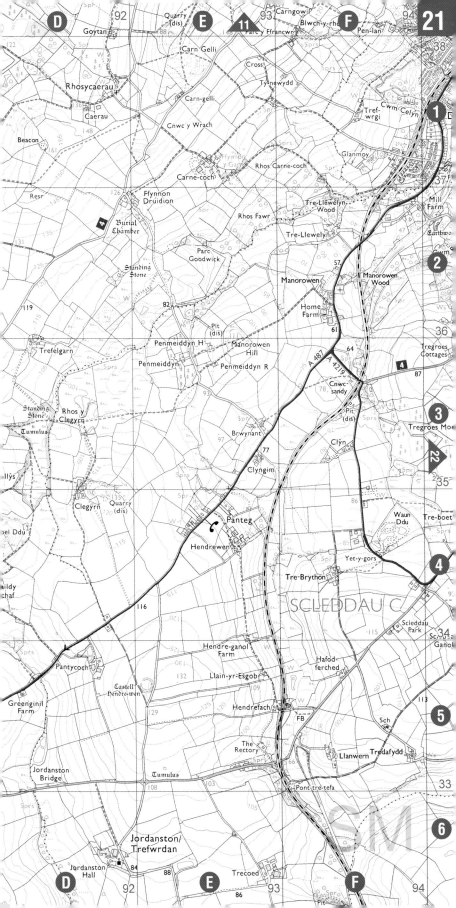

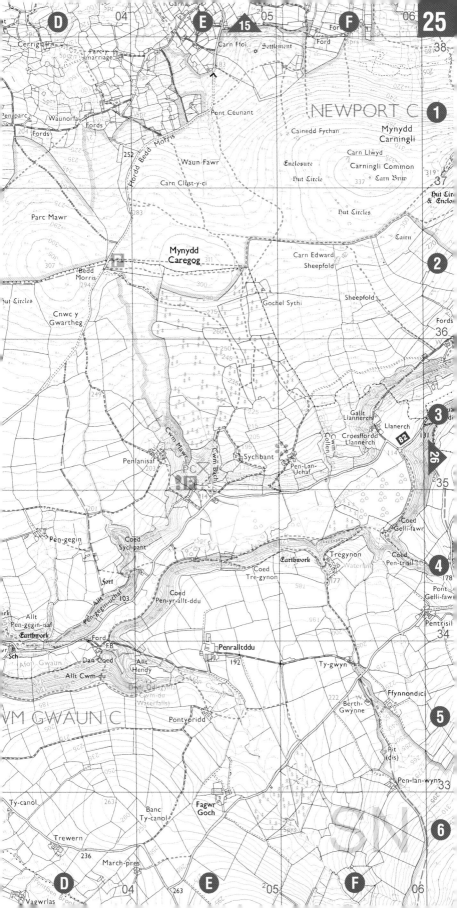

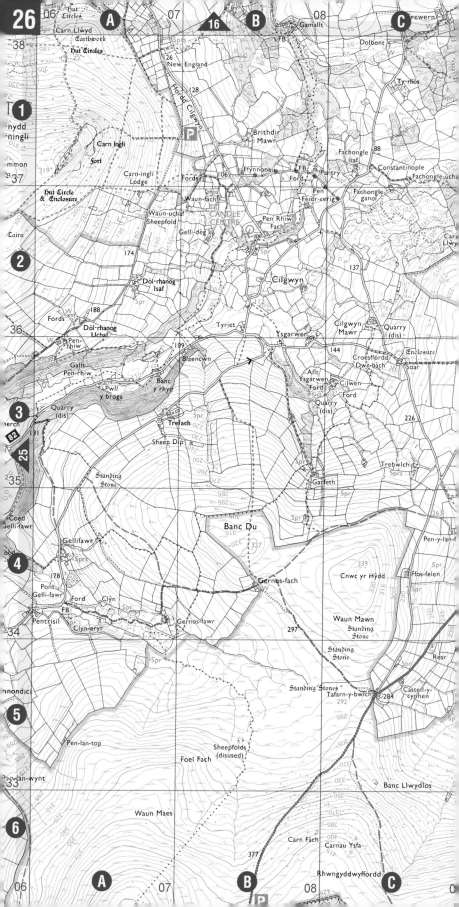

❶
32

❷
31

❸
²30

❹
29

❺
28

Carn Porth-llong

Llechenhinen

Ogof Coetan

Coetan Arthur
Burial Chamber

Ogof Crisial   Spr

Ogof Gefr   fort
(Caves)

Porthmelgan

St Davids Head/   Certhios
Penmaen Dewi   Porth-melgan   Cave

Penlledwen

❻   Craig y Cre

Po

Trwynhwre

Whitesands Bay
Porth Mawr
27

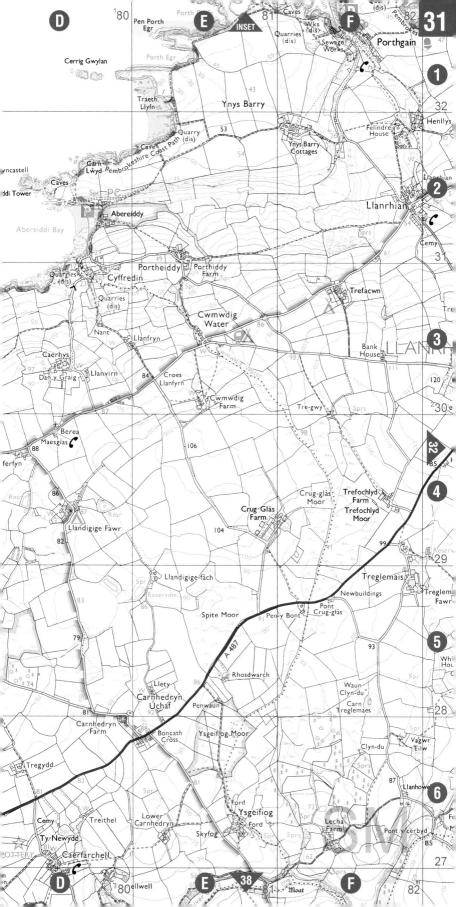

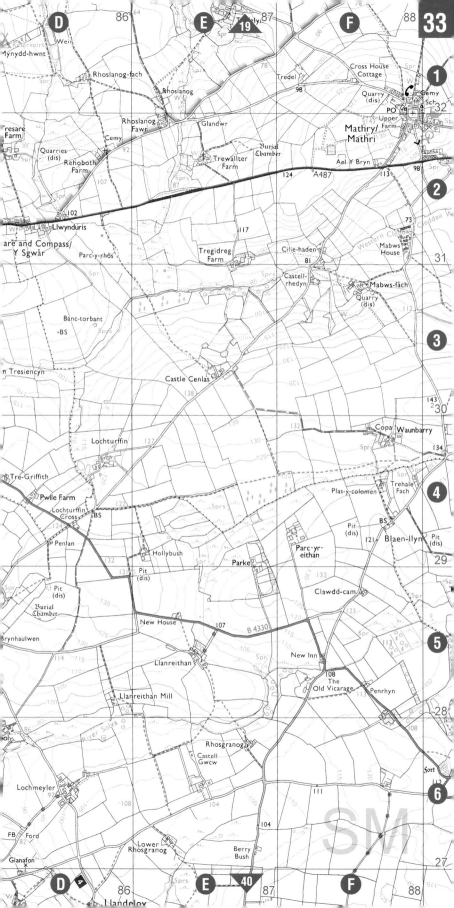

67 A 68 B 69 C

27

1

26

24
22

Clerks

2
Carreg Rhoson

and

²25

Bishops

Cave

Trwyn-drain-du

Ogof Ty
(Cave
Ogo
(C

Car
Lludw
Brwd

Llechau-Uchaf

3

The Ovens

Aber Mawr

Trwyn
Garlic

24

Trwynllundain

Moelyn

Llechau-isaf

Ramsey Island
Nature Reserve

Ogof
Colomennod

Rams

Trwyn
Bendro

Cader
Rhwydog

Sp

Pwll Bendro

13

136

Carreg-gwylan

Carnllundain
Cairn 128

4

Trwyn yr Allt

Ogof
Glyma

100

23

Allt Felin-fawr

Porth
Lleuog

Bancyn-ffald

9
Trwynmynach

5

22

6

Meini Duon 6

10

67 A 68 B 69 C

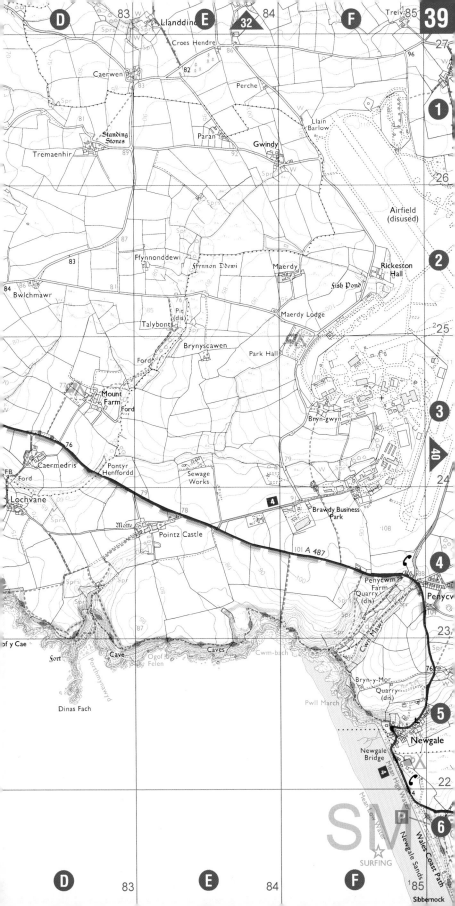

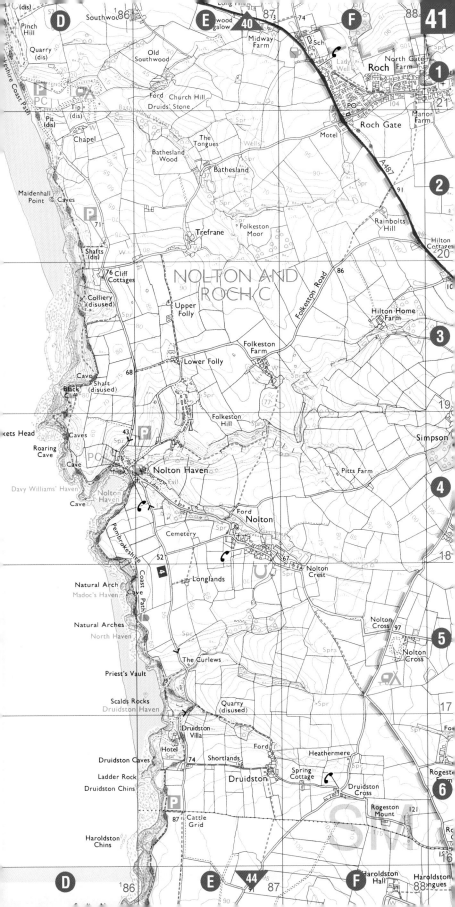

79 **A** ¹80 **B** 81 **C**

16

1

²15

2

14

3

Stack Rocks
25

13

Brandy Bay
Dutch Gin
Foxes' Holes
Mill Haven
Sort
40

4

Cave
Lower Broadmoor

12

Halfway Rock
Pump House
Warey Haven
48
Ripperston Farm
Sprs

5

Pembrokeshire Coast Path
The Falls
Enclosu
Upper Ripperston Farm
57

The Nab Head
Siver
Huntsman's Leap
Castle Head
Sort
Wales Coast Path
St Brides H
Cliff Cottage
St Brides Cross
Windmill Park
61

11

Cave
wer
int

Sort
32
Castle
St Brides Green
40
60
55

6

P PC
9

79 **A** ¹80 **49** **B** St Brides 81 **C**

Resr
.62
The Moors
St Brides
Pearson Farm
99

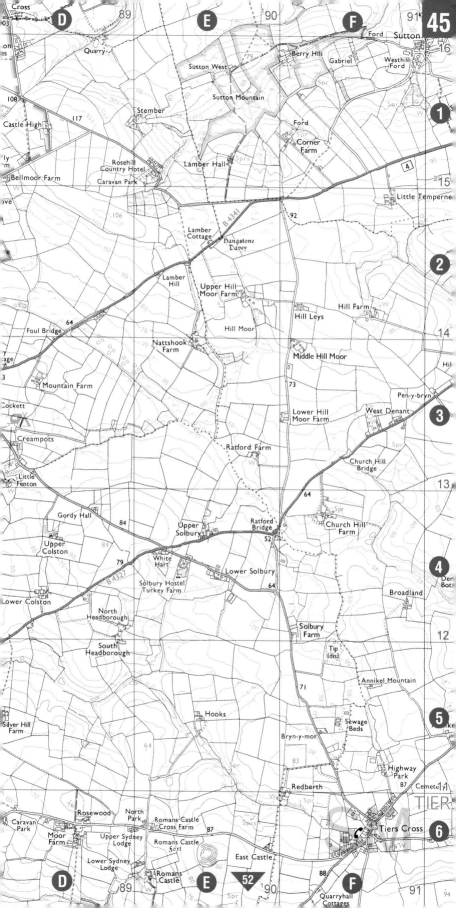

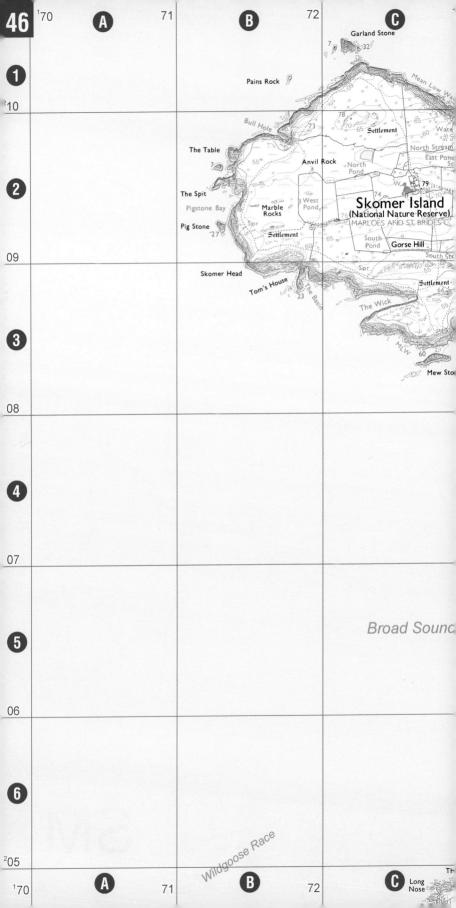

Garland Stone

Pains Rock

Bull Hole

The Table

Anvil Rock

North Stream

Settlement

East Pond

The Spit

North Pond

The Spit

Pigstone Bay

Marble Rocks

West Pond

Skomer Island
(National Nature Reserve)
MARLOES AND ST. BRIDES

Pig Stone

Settlement

South Pond

Gorse Hill

South Str

Skomer Head

Spr

Settlement

Tom's House

The Basin

The Wick

Mew Sto

MLW

Broad Sound

Wildgoose Race

Long Nose

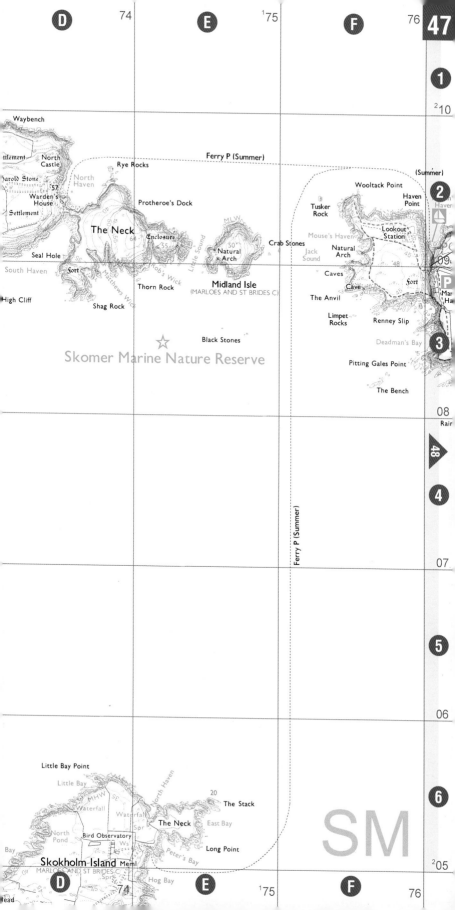

1

²10

Waybench

Ferry P (Summer)

Rye Rocks

(Summer)

Settlement
North
Castle

North
Haven

Wooltack Point

Haven
Point

Harold Stone

57

Tusker
Rock

Haven

2

Warden's
House

Protheroe's Dock

Lookout
Station

Settlement

MLW

Mouse's Haven

The Neck

Crab Stones

Natural
Arch

Jack
Sound

Enclosure

64

55

Natural
Arch

48

45

09

Seal Hole

50

Little Sound

Fort

South Haven

Fort

Rob's Wick

Midland Isle
(MARLOES AND ST BRIDES C.)

Caves

Fort

P

Mar
Ha

Thorn Rock

Cave

High Cliff

Matthews Wick

Shag Rock

The Anvil

Renney Slip

3

Limpet
Rocks

☆

Black Stones

Deadman's Bay

Skomer Marine Nature Reserve

Pitting Gales Point

The Bench

08

Rair

◄**48**

4

Ferry P (Summer)

07

5

06

Little Bay Point

Little Bay

North Haven

6

Waterfall

The Stack

20

Waterfall

Spr

The Neck

East Bay

SM

North
Pond

Bird Observatory

Ws

Bay

Long Point

Peter's Bay

Skokholm Island Meml
(MARLOES AND ST BRIDES C.)

45

Spr

Hog Bay

²05

48

76 A 77 B 78 C

1

10

(Summer)

Point Martin's
Haven

High Point

Howney Stone

Quarry Pit

2

Musselwick Sands

Black Cliff

PC

Inscribed Stone

West Hook Farm

East Hook
Farm

Hopgang

Pembrokeshire Coast Path

09

Fort

P

Martin's
Haven

46

Treehill
Farm

68

Marloes
Beacon

3

59

69

72

76

Slip

60

51

63

Marloes
Court
House

Point

45

52

P

PC

Marloes Mere

Marloes
Court
Farm

ranch

Fort

49

Runwayskiln

08

Rainy Rock

Little Castle Bay

Victoria Bay

Watery Bay

Cave

The Pits

Green Mire
Cottage

47

Raggle
Rocks

FB

51

4

Albion Sands

Gateholm
Stack

Mean High Water

Cave

Little Ma
Farr

Marloes Sands

FB

MHW

Mean Low Water

Waterfall

Settlement

Cairn

Gateholm Island

07

5

Hooper's Point

06

6

05

76 A 77 B 78 C

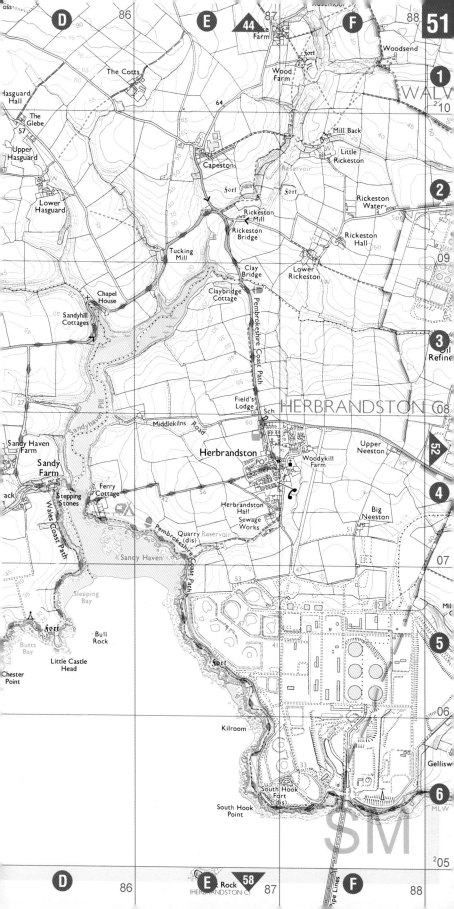

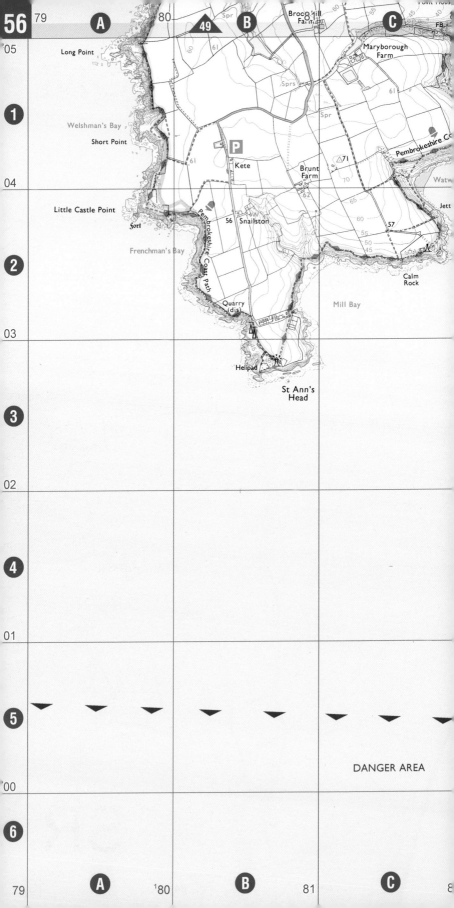

79 A 80 49 B Broco Hill Farm C FB

Long Point

Maryborough Farm

Spr

1

Welshman's Bay

Short Point

Pembrokeshire Co

Spr

P

Kete

Brunt Farm

04

Little Castle Point

56 Snailston

Jett

Fort

Frenchman's Bay

2

Calm Rock

Quarry (dis)

Mill Bay

03

Helipad

St Ann's Head

3

02

4

01

5

DANGER AREA

00

6

79 A 80 B 81 C 8

SM

Castlebeach Bay

Watwick Point

Blockhouse Point

Thorn Island (ANGLE C) Hotel

West Angle Bay

Lowrey's Rock

East Block House (remains of) Rat Island

51
46
53
52
58
40
45

Pembrokeshire Coast Path

Castles Bay
Fort
49
51
50
Whitedole Bay

Sheep Island

Parsonsquarry Bay

Gu (Nat

SR

205
04
03
02
01
200

1
2
3
4
5
6

²05

Man of War **SM** Roads

1

Pipe Lines

Jetty

Jetties

Pipe Lines

berdaugleddyf

04

Popton Point

Bullwell Bay

Cave

Fort Popton

Fort

2

Oil Refinery

59

48

Sawdern Point

Sawdern

Pembrokeshire Coast Path

03

Chy

Angle Bay

MLW

18

Eastington and remains of Manor House

3

63

Rhoscrowther

MHW

St Deqman's Well

Sprs

02

West Coast Path

Chever

39

Sprs

4

Spr

Broomhill

35 40

Middlehill

Resr

Sprs

Neath Bridge

Neath

Vi Cot

Broomhill Cottage

01

B 4319

B 4320

Dunes

The Devil's Quoit Burial Chamber

War Meml

Tumulus

Kilpaison Burrows

Dunes

P Dunes

Broomhill Burrows

12

Pit (dis)

The Hoary Rocks

Dunes

Newton

5

Harry Standup

63

Tel Ex

Pembrokeshire Coast Path

reshwater West

Pit (dis)

Newton Burrows

36

²00

SR

Dunes

Starmans Hall

6

Little Furzenip

P

24 89 6

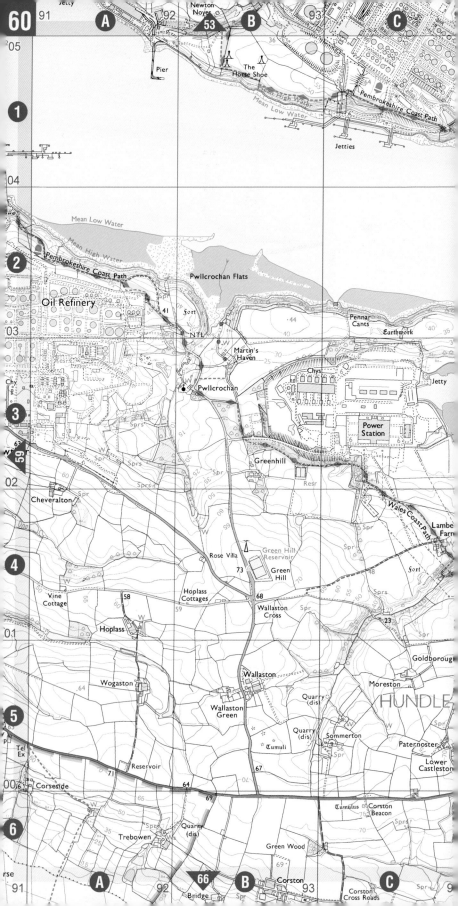

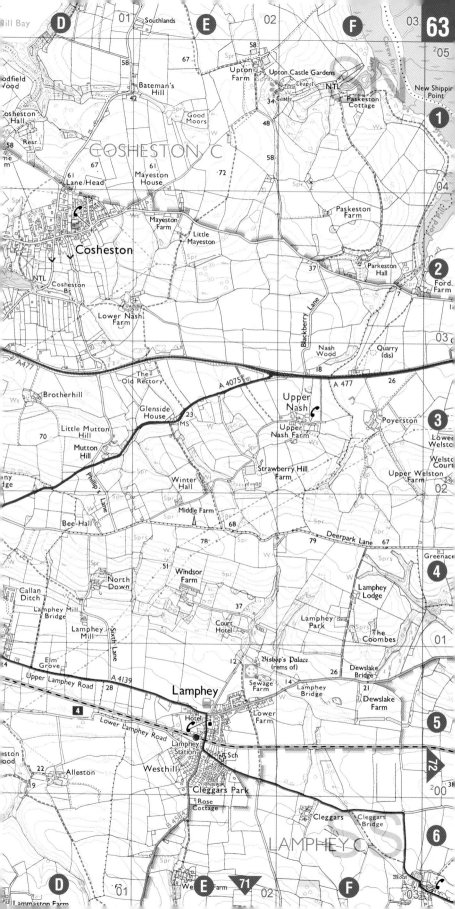

1

99

2

DANGER AREA

98

3

97

Brimstone P

H

4

96

5

¹95

6

94

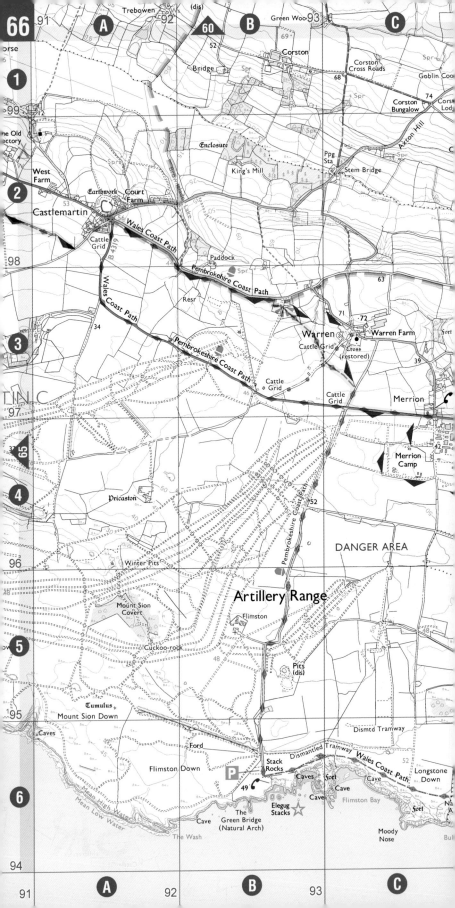

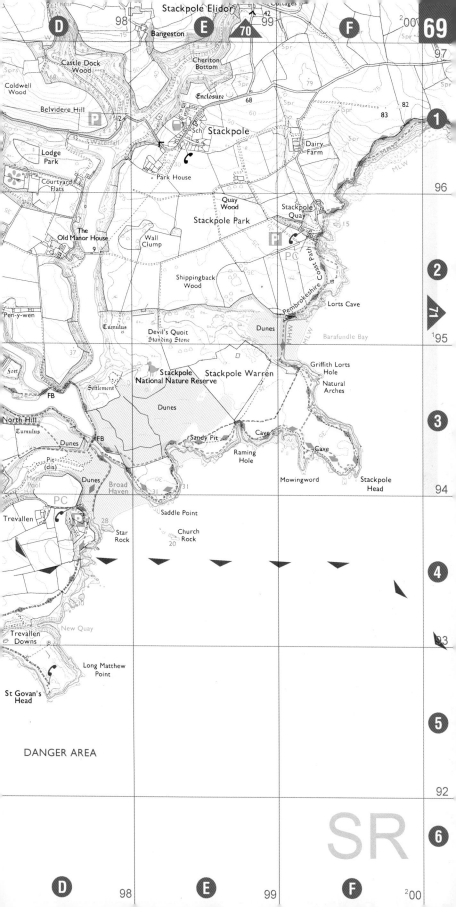

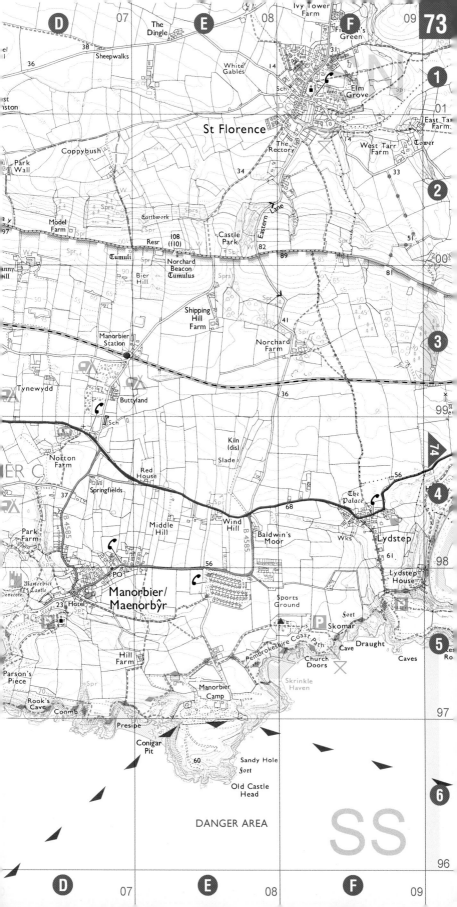

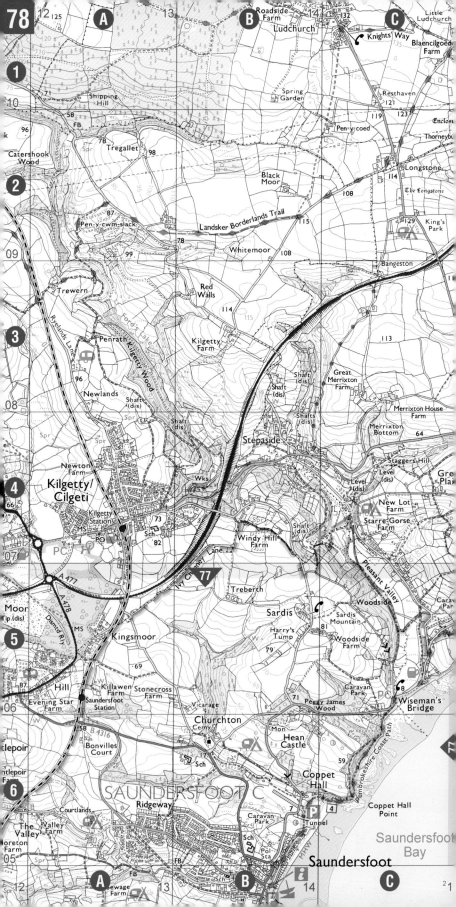

1. The map reference given refers to the actual square in which the feature is located and not the name.

2. A strict alphabetical order is used e.g. Trwyncastell follows Trwyn Bendro but precedes Trwyn Cynddeiriog

3. Names prefixed with 'The' are indexed under the main name, for example 'The Anvil' appears in the A section.

THE NATIONAL GRID REFERENCING SYSTEM

The grid lines form part of the National Grid and are at 1 km intervals.

To give a unique reference position of a point to within 100 metres proceed as follows:

Sample point: **Abercastle**

1. Read letters identifying 100,000 metre square in which the point lies (**SM**)

2. FIRST QUOTE EASTINGS - locate the first VERTICAL grid line to LEFT of the point and read the BLUE figures labelling the line in the top or bottom margin of the page (**85**). Estimate tenths from the grid line to the point (**3**). This gives a figure of **853**

3. THEN QUOTE NORTHINGS - locate the first HORIZONTAL grid line BELOW the point and read the BLUE figures labelling the line in the left or right margin of the page (**33**). Estimate tenths from the grid line to the point (**5**). This gives a figure of **335**

Sample Reference: **Abercastle SM 853 335**

Aber Bach	.6F **13**	SM 995 388
	.3A **20**	SM 883 350
Abercastle	.5D **19**	SM 853 335
Aberdaugleddau	.6C **52**	SM 904 057
Aberdinas	.3B **30**	SM 775 305
Aber Draw	.6B **18**	SM 832 326
Abereiddi Bay	.2D **31**	SM 795 312
Abereiddi Car Park	.2D **31**	SM 797 312
Abereiddy	.2D **31**	SM 798 313
Aber Felin	.4E **11**	SM 928 402
Aberfelin	.4D **35**	SM 706 235
Abergwaun	.1B **22**	SM 955 377
Aber Mawr	.3C **34**	SM 698 242
Aber-mawr	.4A **20**	SM 880 347
Aber Pensidan	.4F **13**	SM 999 407
Aber-pwll	.3C **30**	SM 784 306
Aber Step	.5D **15**	SM 037 399
Aberteifi	.3C **8**	SN 178 461
Aber-west	.4C **38**	SM 811 232
Aber Yw	.5D **19**	SM 855 338
Afon Brynberian	.2F **27**	SN 115 366
Afon Gwaun	.2D **23**	SM 975 365
Afon Nyfer	.5A **16**	SN 066 394
	.1F **27**	SN 119 372
Afon Teifi	.3B **8**	SN 167 460
Albion Sands	.4B **48**	SM 770 074
Allt Felin-fawr	.5C **34**	SM 694 229
Allt Pontfaen Car Park	.5C **24**	SN 024 339
Allt-y-goed	.1B **6**	SN 135 494
Allt-y-goed Car Park	.1B **6**	SN 134 492
Amroth	.4E **79**	SN 163 070
Amroth Car Park	.4E **79**	SN 162 070
Anglas Bay	.4A **12**	SM 946 404
Angle	.3B **58**	SM 864 029
Angle Bay	.3D **59**	SM 881 025
Angle Point	.2C **58**	SM 875 032
The Anvil	.3F **47**	SM 754 088
Axton Hill	.2C **66**	SR 935 987
Bae Abergwaun	.5D **13**	SM 971 392
Bae Trefdraeth	.4D **15**	SN 031 409
Banc Du	.4B **26**	SN 073 347
Bancyn-ffald	.5C **34**	SM 693 228
Banc-y-Warren	.2F **9**	SN 204 475
Barafundle Bay	.2F **69**	SR 993 950
Barrack Hill	.2E **61**	SM 956 031
The Basin	.3B **46**	SM 719 088
Bastleford Bridge	.2B **54**	SM 950 095
Bay Dillyn	.5D **35**	SM 704 223
Bedd Morris	.2D **25**	SN 037 364
Bedd Morris Car Park	.2D **25**	SN 038 365
Begelly	.4A **78**	SN 118 073
Belvidere Hill	.1D **69**	SR 973 965
The Bench	.3F **47**	SM 756 082
The Bennett	.4F **15**	SN 053 403
Benton Wood	.4F **55**	SN 000 073
Berry Slade	.4D **65**	SR 883 969
Bishops and Clerks	.3A **34**	SM 668 248
The Bitches	.4D **35**	SM 707 236
Black Bridge	.5D **53**	SM 916 061
Black Cave	.5B **58**	SM 869 007
Black Cliff	.3D **41**	SM 855 191
Black Point	.1A **44**	SM 858 153
Black Scar	.5A **38**	SM 792 225
Black Stones	.3E **47**	SM 747 085
Black Tar	.2F **55**	SM 997 095

Black Tar Car Park	.2F **55**	SM 998
Blacktar Point	.2F **55**	SM 997
Blucks Pool	.3D **65**	SR 885
Boncath Cross	.6E **31**	SM 801
Borough Head	.4E **43**	SM 836
Bosherston	.3C **68**	SM 966
Bosherston Car Park	.3C **68**	SR 966
Bosherston Lily Ponds	.3C **68**	SR 969
Brawdy Business Park	.4F **39**	SM 841
Bridgend	.4C **8**	SN 177
Broadfield	.4E **77**	SN 130
Broad Haven	.3A **44**	SM 859
	.3B **44**	SM 863
	.3D **69**	SR 978
Broad Haven, Marine Road Car Park	.3B **44**	SM 860
Broad Haven, Millmoor Car Park	.2B **44**	SM 861
Broad Haven South Car Park	.4D **69**	SR 976
Broad Haven Youth Hostel	.2B **44**	SM 862
Broadmoor	.1A **76**	SN 095
Broad Sound	.5C **46**	SM 724
Broadway	.3C **44**	SM 875
Broomhill Burrows	.5D **59**	SM 885
Brownslade Burrows	.2E **65**	SR 892
Brynberian	.3E **27**	SN 102
Bryn-henllan	.5B **14**	SN 010
Buckspool Down	.4B **68**	SR 954
Bull Hole	.2B **46**	SM 716
Bulliber Down	.5F **65**	SR 905
Bullslaughter Bay	.6C **66**	SR 939
Bullwell Bay	.2F **59**	SM 900
The Burrows	.3D **75**	SS 124
Burton	.6E **55**	SM 984
Burton Ferry	.6D **55**	SM 978
Burton Mountain	.6F **55**	SM 991
Bushford Bridge	.1B **50**	SM 836
Bwlch y groes	.2F **17**	SN 110
Bwn Bach	.5A **6**	SN 094
Caer Bwdy Bay	.3D **37**	SM 765
Caerfai Bay	.3C **36**	SM 758
Caerfai Bay Car Park	.3C **36**	SM 759
Caerfarchell	.6D **31**	SM 794
Cafnau	.4F **13**	SM 999
Caldey Island	.6E **75**	SS 138
Caldey Island Museum	.6F **75**	SS 141
Caldey Point	.6F **75**	SS 149
Caldey Roads	.5E **75**	SS 134
Caldey Sound	.5C **74**	SS 118
Cardigan	.3C **8**	SN 178
Cardigan Information Centre	.3C **8**	SN 178
Careg Aderyn	.1B **6**	SN 135
Carew River	.1F **63**	SN 027
Carn ar Wig	.4E **35**	SM 718
Carnedd-Lleithr	.5E **29**	SM 747
Carn Fran	.1D **23**	SM 977
Carn Ingli	.1A **26**	SN 064
Carn Ingli Car Park	.1B **26**	SN 070
Carningli Common	.1F **25**	SN 055
Carn Llidi Bychan	.6D **29**	SM 735
Carnllundain	.4C **34**	SM 696
Carn Perfedd	.5E **29**	SM 749
Carn Treliwyd	.5F **29**	SM 752
Carnysgubor	.3C **34**	SM 699
Carreg Bica	.5A **6**	SN 091
Carreg Coetan	.5A **16**	SN 062
Carregedrywy	.3E **15**	SN 046

reg Fran ....5A **36** SM 731 229
reg-gafeiliog ....1E **35** SM 719 263
reg Golchfa ....3A **20** SM 881 352
reg-gwylan ....4C **34** SM 692 234
reg-gwylan-fach ....3B **30** SM 772 304
reg Gybi ....3C **10** SM 903 412
reg Herefio ....2A **20** SM 880 360
reg Onnen ....3A **10** SM 888 411
reg Onnen Bay ....4B **10** SM 892 409
reg Rhoson ....2A **34** SM 668 255
regwastad Point ....4E **11** SM 926 406
reg Wylan ....4B **6** SN 104 457
reg y Barcud ....3E **37** SM 770 240
reg yr Afr ....4F **29** SM 758 291
reg yr Esgob ....4F **35** SM 728 231
reg Yspar ....4A **6** SN 098 450
's Rock ....1E **61** SM 955 041
tell Henllys ....5F **17** SN 117 390
tell-Mawr ....1F **27** SN 118 377
Castle ....4B **68** SR 953 933
tlebeach Bay ....1D **57** SM 820 048
tle Dock Wood Car Park ....1D **69** SM 979 965
tlemartin ....2A **66** SR 915 983
tle Pill ....6D **53** SM 915 057
tle Point ....1C **22** SM 961 378
tles Bay ....4F **57** SM 844 019
Rock ....5E **15** SN 040 399
owr Bay ....4B **6** SN 108 458
Howel ....1C **16** SN 085 435
naes Head ....1B **6** SN 131 501
naes Head Nature Reserve ..1B **6** SN 133 498
rig Duon ....5F **13** SM 996 391
rig Gwylan ....1D **31** SM 796 322
ig duon ....4F **15** SN 052 406
pel Bay ....2B **58** SM 861 036
pel Hill ....2E **67** SM 957 981
pel Hill Bridge ....3E **67** SR 956 979
pel Point ....6F **75** SS 142 957
eriton ....3B **70** SM 988 972
rch Hill ....1E **41** SM 863 210
rch Hill Bridge ....3F **45** SM 904 132
rch Rock ....4E **69** SM 982 937
rchton ....2E **77** SN 132 059
jeti ....4A **78** SN 123 073
gwyn ....2B **26** SN 078 363
hedyn Bridge ....4A **24** SN 005 348
hedyn Bridge Car Park .....4A **24** SN 005 348
pin Stone ....5E **15** SN 046 393
pyn ....2F **7** SN 140 478
y Bridge ....3E **51** SM 867 089
ddau Bridge ....1A **62** SM 974 048
ggars Bridge ....6F **63** SS 024 999
ggars Park ....5E **63** SN 015 001
gyr-Boia ....2A **36** SM 737 250
cheston Pill ....2B **62** SM 984 036
ch y Ceiliog ....1D **23** SM 970 379
ed Cwm Gloyne ....5E **17** SN 105 396
ed Maidie B. Goddard Nature Reserve
...........................6F **9** SN 209 436
edmor National Nature Reserve .6E **9** SN 195 435
by Woodland Garden ....3D **79** SN 157 080
by Woodland Garden Car Park .3D **79** SN 158 080
d Inn ....2B **76** SN 102 055
d Inn Cross ....2B **76** SN 102 056
nnermoor Bridge ....6D **43** SM 822 109
ppet Hall ....2E **77** SN 139 054
ppet Hall Car Park ....2E **77** SN 139 053
ppet Hall Point ....2F **77** SN 142 054
rnish Down ....6C **76** SN 117 019
rston Cross Roads ....1C **66** SR 931 992
sheston ....2D **63** SN 005 036
sheston Point ....1B **62** SM 983 040
e Cradle ....4F **37** SM 789 236
ckmail Down ....3A **68** SR 943 940
ncoed Point ....4B **12** SM 951 402
ney Bridge ....3D **23** SM 973 358
terion Way Car Park ....2F **61** SM 968 038
ies-goch ....3A **32** SM 828 302
ies Hendre ....1E **39** SM 835 269
ies Llanfyrn ....3E **31** SM 801 302
ies-y-Llan ....4E **9** SN 198 452
ow Cwm ....4B **40** SM 864 238
ow Rock ....6D **65** SR 886 947
rm ....1F **9** SN 207 492
...........................1C **22** SM 963 371
m Bach ....3E **25** SN 045 352
rm-bach ....5E **39** SM 838 229
rm Collen ....3F **25** SN 053 353
rm Degwel ....4B **8** SN 161 452
rm Gwaun ....2D **23** SM 975 365
...........................4A **24** SN 007 347

Cwm-mawr ....3E **25** SN 042 354
Cwm Trewyddel ....4C **6** SN 112 453
Cwmwdig Water ....3E **31** SM 805 305
Cwm-yr-Eglwys ....4B **14** SN 014 400
Cwm-yr-Eglwys Car Park ....4B **14** SN 014 400
Cwm yr Esgyr ....1E **7** SN 132 480
Cyffredin ....3D **31** SM 798 309

Dale ....6F **49** SM 810 056
Dale Car Park ....6F **49** SM 811 058
Dale Point ....6A **50** SM 824 051
Dale Roads ....6A **50** SM 821 058
Deadman's Bay ....3F **47** SM 759 085
Deerland ....1E **55** SM 984 104
Den Point ....5F **75** SS 145 970
The Devil's Quoit ....5D **59** SM 886 008
Dewslake Bridge ....5F **63** SN 026 007
Dinas Cross ....6A **14** SN 005 385
Dinas Fach ....5D **39** SM 825 225
Dinas Fawr ....4C **38** SM 811 230
Dinas Head ....3A **14** SN 004 413
Dinas Island ....4A **14** SN 005 404
Dinbych-y-Pysgod ....2E **75** SN 132 005
Dirty Corner ....2C **54** SM 963 094
Doc Penfro ....2E **61** SM 956 037
The Downs ....3C **70** SR 996 978
Dowrog Common ....6B **30** SM 770 270
Dowrog Common Nature Reserve .1E **37** SM 771 269
Drinkim ....6F **75** SS 146 962
Druidston ....6E **41** SM 869 166
Druidston Cross ....6F **41** SM 873 164
Druidston Haven ....5D **41** SM 859 170
Dyffryn ....1A **22** SM 940 375

East Bay ....6E **47** SM 745 053
East Moor Cliff ....5B **72** SS 046 975
East Pickard Bay ....5B **58** SM 862 008
East Trewent ....3D **71** SS 008 973
East Williamston ....2A **76** SN 096 050
Eel Point ....5E **75** SS 130 972
Elegug Stacks ....6B **66** SR 926 944
Esgyrn Bottom ....4C **22** SM 967 343

The Falls ....5B **42** SM 804 113
Felindre Farchog ....5E **17** SN 100 390
Ferry Hill ....5F **55** SN 000 063
Fishguard ....1B **22** SM 955 377
Fishguard & Goodwick Station .6A **12** SM 945 382
Fishguard Bay ....5D **13** SM 971 392
Fishguard Fort Car Park ...1C **22** SM 962 376
Fishguard Harbour ....6B **12** SM 952 384
Fishguard Harbour Information Centre
...........................1A **22** SM 947 379
Fishguard Harbour Station .6B **12** SM 951 389
Fishguard Information Centre .2B **22** SM 958 369
Flimston Bay ....6C **66** SR 931 944
Flimston Down ....6A **66** SR 917 946
Foel Fach ....2F **15** SN 056 421
Foel Goch ....1B **16** SN 071 430
Folkeston Hill ....4E **41** SM 865 189
Foul Bridge ....2D **45** SM 885 140
Frainslake Sands ....2D **65** SR 888 982
Frenchman's Bay ....2B **56** SM 800 035
Freshwater East ....2E **71** SS 017 983
...........................3F **71** SS 021 978
Freshwater East Car Park ..3E **71** SS 014 981
Freshwater West ....5D **59** SM 881 000
Freshwater West Car Park (North) ..5D **59** SM 884 004
Freshwater West Car Park (South) ..6D **59** SR 885 995

Garland Stone ....1C **46** SM 721 104
Garn Fawr ....6B **10** SM 895 388
Garn Fawr Car Park ....6B **10** SM 898 388
Gateholm Island ....4A **48** SM 769 071
Gateholm Stack ....4B **48** SM 771 074
Gelliswick Bay ....6A **52** SM 887 054
Gesail-fawr ....5E **29** SM 741 288
Gethsemane ....3B **16** SN 074 419
Gewni ....4A **38** SM 796 235
Giltar Point ....4D **75** SS 125 982
Glanpwllafon ....6C **8** SN 178 437
Glanpwllafon Bridge ....6C **8** SN 179 437
Glenowen ....6B **54** SM 954 058
Godir-y-bwch ....2F **15** SN 052 425
Golden Hill ....3B **62** SM 988 022
Goodwick ....6A **12** SM 944 382
Goodwick Moor Car Park ....1A **22** SM 949 376

Place	Ref	Page	Grid
Goodwick Moor Nature Reserve	1A	**22**	SM 945 374
Gorse Hill	2C	**46**	SM 724 091
Goultrop Roads	4F	**43**	SM 841 126
Granston	4B	**20**	SM 896 341
Gravel Bay	5C	**58**	SM 876 005
Great Castle Head	6D	**49**	SR 797 056
	6C	**50**	SM 848 058
Great Furzenip	2D	**65**	SR 886 986
Great Honeyborough	5C	**54**	SM 962 060
Green	4B	**62**	SM 985 018
The Green	2D	**75**	SN 126 008
Greenala Point	4D	**71**	SS 007 965
The Green Bridge	6B	**66**	SR 924 944
Green Grove	4C	**72**	SS 054 989
Green Scar	5A	**38**	SM 796 226
Grove	5B	**62**	SM 989 009
Guildford	2F	**55**	SM 991 091
Gumfreston	1B	**74**	SN 108 012
Gupton Burrows	1D	**65**	SM 886 994
Guttle Hole	4A	**58**	SM 854 011
Gwahan	1D	**35**	SM 706 260
Gwrhyd Mawr	6A	**30**	SM 767 276
Hakin	6B	**52**	SM 892 057
Half Tide Rock	5B	**36**	SM 741 227
Halfway Rock	5B	**42**	SM 807 119
Hamilton Backpackers Lodge	2B	**22**	SM 958 369
Hanging Tar	4D	**65**	SR 881 966
Harmeston Cross	2E	**53**	SM 925 095
Harmony	6C	**10**	SM 901 382
Haroldston Bridge	1A	**44**	SM 858 154
	3B	**44**	SM 861 139
Haroldston Chins	6D	**41**	SM 859 161
Haroldston Chins Car Park	6E	**41**	SM 862 163
Haroldston West	1B	**44**	SM 866 154
Hasguard Cross	6F	**43**	SM 849 107
Haven Point	2F	**47**	SM 759 093
Hayston Bridge	3F	**53**	SM 935 087
Hazelbeach	1D	**61**	SM 947 048
The Head	6D	**47**	SM 730 048
Henner Cross	6F	**11**	SM 931 387
Herbrandston	4E	**51**	SM 869 076
High Cliff	5F	**75**	SS 144 971
High Point	2A	**48**	SM 768 092
Hill Mountain	3D	**55**	SM 976 083
Hobbs Point	1F	**61**	SM 967 042
Hodgeston	1F	**71**	SS 029 994
Hog Bay	6E	**47**	SM 741 049
Holloway Bridge	2C	**74**	SN 118 003
Hooper's Point	5C	**48**	SM 787 063
The Horse Shoe	1B	**60**	SM 924 047
Houghton	4E	**55**	SM 983 072
Howney Stone	4D	**43**	SM 820 128
	2B	**48**	SM 776 091
Hubberston	5B	**52**	SM 892 063
Hubberston Pill	5C	**52**	SM 901 066
Hundleton	5F	**61**	SM 961 006
Huntsman's Leap	5A	**42**	SM 795 112
Iron Point	6D	**49**	SM 797 053
Jack Sound	2F	**47**	SM 751 090
Jameston	3C	**72**	SS 056 990
Jeffreyston	1A	**76**	SN 089 065
Johnston	1F	**53**	SM 932 104
Johnston Station	1F	**53**	SM 932 106
Jordanston	6D	**21**	SM 918 326
Jordanston Bridge	5D	**21**	SM 912 330
Kete Car Park	1B	**56**	SM 803 042
Kilgetty	4A	**78**	SN 123 073
Kilgetty Station	4A	**78**	SN 126 072
Kilpaison Burrows	5E	**59**	SM 893 006
Kilroom	6E	**51**	SM 868 059
Kingsbridge	4C	**62**	SM 995 014
Kingsmoor	1D	**77**	SN 124 065
Kings Street	6A	**16**	SN 060 388
Kingston Hill	1B	**70**	SR 987 993
Lady Park	6D	**77**	SN 125 015
Lake	2F	**71**	SS 023 988
Lamphey	5E	**63**	SN 015 005
Lamphey Bishop's Palace	5E	**63**	SN 018 009
Lamphey Bridge	5F	**63**	SN 020 007
Lamphey Mill Bridge	4D	**63**	SN 006 012
Lamphey Station	5E	**63**	SN 014 003
Leonardston	6A	**54**	SM 949
Liddeston	5B	**52**	SM 895
Lindsway Bay	5C	**50**	SM 842
Linney Burrows	3E	**65**	SR 892
Linney Head	5D	**65**	SR 883
Little Bay Point	6D	**47**	SM 737
Little Castle Head	5D	**51**	SM 854
Little Castle Point	2A	**56**	SM 797
Little Furzenip	1D	**65**	SR 884
Little Haven	4A	**44**	SM 855
Little Haven Car Park	4A	**44**	SM 856
Little Honeyborough	5B	**54**	SM 950
Little Sound	2E	**47**	SM 744
Llandeloy	1A	**40**	SM 858
Llandruidion	3F	**37**	SM 784
Llandudoch	3B	**8**	SN 162
Llangloffan	6C	**20**	SM 905
Llangloffan Cross	6C	**20**	SM 905
Llangwm	2F	**55**	SM 993
Llanion	1A	**62**	SM 972
Llanon	2B	**32**	SM 838
Llanreath	2E	**61**	SM 952
Llanrhian	2F	**31**	SM 819
Llanstadwell	6B	**54**	SM 955
Llanteg	1F	**79**	SN 181
Llanteglos	2F	**79**	SN 175
Llanwnda	5F	**11**	SM 933
Llanychaer	3E	**23**	SM 987
Llechaucochion	3A	**30**	SM 767
Llechau-isaf	4B	**34**	SM 680
Llechau-uchaf	3B	**34**	SM 682
Llech Dafad	3A	**20**	SM 880
Llechenhinen	5C	**28**	SM 726
Llech Uchaf	1C	**30**	SM 788
Lochturffin Cross	4D	**33**	SM 855
Lochvane	4D	**39**	SM 821
Longhouse	5C	**18**	SM 846
Long Matthew Point	5D	**69**	SR 976
Long Nose	6C	**46**	SM 727
Long Point	6E	**47**	SM 744
	1A	**56**	SM 795
Longstone	2C	**78**	SN 145
Longstone Down	6C	**66**	SR 936
Lower Kingheriot	1B	**38**	SM 809
Lower Moor	2B	**36**	SM 747
Lower Solva	3B	**38**	SM 807
Lower Town	1C	**22**	SM 963
Lower Town Car Park	1C	**22**	SM 962
Ludchurch	1C	**78**	SN 141
Lydstep	4F	**73**	SS 085
Lydstep Haven	4A	**74**	SS 093
Lydstep Haven Car Park	5F	**73**	SS 088
Lydstep Point	5A	**74**	SS 093
Mad Bay	6D	**47**	SM 731
Madoc's Haven	5D	**41**	SM 857
Maen Bachau	3F	**35**	SM 722
Maidenhall Point	2D	**41**	SM 854
Maiden Wells	6A	**62**	SR 972
Man of War Roads	1F	**59**	SM 901
Manorbier	5D	**73**	SS 066
Manorbier Bay	5C	**72**	SS 056
Manorbier Car Park	5D	**73**	SS 064
Manorbier Castle	5D	**73**	SS 063
Manorbier Newton	2B	**72**	SN 045
Manorbier Station	3D	**73**	SS 069
Manorbier Youth Hostel	5F	**73**	SS 080
Manor House Wildlife Park	5A	**76**	SN 089
Manorowen Hill	3E	**21**	SM 927
The Mare	5A	**38**	SM 799
Marloes	3D	**49**	SM 792
Marloes Beacon	3C	**48**	SM 785
Marloes Sands	4C	**48**	SM 781
Marloes Sands Car Park	3B	**48**	SM 779
Marloes Sands Youth Hostel	3B	**48**	SM 778
Martin's Haven	2A	**48**	SM 760
Martin's Haven Car Park	3A	**48**	SM 761
Mascle Bridge	6B	**54**	SM 954
Mathri	2F	**33**	SM 879
Mathry	2F	**33**	SM 879
Meini Duon	6C	**34**	SM 695
Merlin's Cross	5C	**62**	SM 994
Merrion	4C	**66**	SR 937
Mesur-y-dorth	3B	**32**	SM 838
Mewsford Point	4A	**68**	SR 942
Mew Stone	3C	**46**	SM 727
Middle Mill	2B	**38**	SM 805
Midland	5D	**35**	SM 705
Midland Isle	3E	**47**	SM 746
Milford Haven	6C	**52**	SM 904

ford Haven Heritage & Maritime Museum	.6C 52	SM 900 059
ford Haven Information Centre	.5B 52	SM 898 062
ford Haven, Marina Car Park	.6C 52	SM 902 056
ford Haven Station	.5B 52	SM 899 062
l Bay	.6F 55	SN 000 050
	.2C 56	SM 810 032
l Haven	.4C 42	SM 815 124
elyn	.4A 34	SM 669 238
nk Haven	.5A 50	SM 828 063
nkstone Beach	.4F 77	SN 146 031
nkstone Point	.4F 77	SN 147 033
nkton	.4A 62	SM 973 014
reton	.2C 76	SM 113 052
unt Sion Down	.5A 66	SR 911 950
wingworth	.3F 69	SR 991 941
ylgrove	.5C 6	SN 117 446
ylgrove Car Park	.5C 6	SN 117 446
llock Bridge	.3F 49	SM 812 083
sselwick Sands	.2C 48	SM 784 090
nydd Caregog	.2E 25	SN 044 365
nydd Carningli	.1F 25	SN 057 373
nydd Cilciffeth	.6B 24	SN 010 324
nydd Dinas	.2A 24	SN 009 368
nydd Melyn	.2C 24	SN 021 362
nydd Morfa	.4F 19	SM 874 341
nydd Preseli	.6F 27	SN 110 326
nydd Tre-newydd	.6C 24	SN 022 322
bb's Bridge	.2C 74	SN 116 005
e Nab Head	.5A 42	SM 790 111
nhyfer	.5C 16	SN 083 399
ath Bridge	.4F 59	SM 904 012
e Neck	.2D 47	SM 737 092
edle Rock	.4B 14	SM 015 409
vern	.5C 16	SN 083 399
w Bridge	.2F 67	SR 965 989
wgale	.5F 39	SM 848 224
wgale Bridge	.5F 39	SM 847 222
wgale Central Car Park	.6A 40	SM 850 217
wgale Maidenhall Car Park	.2D 41	SM 858 201
wgale Sands	.6F 39	SM 848 217
wgale South Car Park	.1D 41	SM 852 211
w Hedges	.5D 77	SN 129 026
wport	.5F 15	SN 057 391
wport Bay	.4D 15	SN 031 409
wport National Park Tourist Information Centre		
	.5F 15	SN 057 392
wport Parrog Car Park	.5F 15	SN 051 396
wport Sands	.4F 15	SN 050 401
wport Sands Car Park	.4F 15	SN 054 405
wport Youth Hostel	.5F 15	SN 058 392
w Shipping Point	.1F 63	SN 029 046
wton Down	.4C 68	SM 960 931
yland	.6C 54	SM 963 051
yland, Station Road Car Park	.1F 61	SM 966 048
e Wells	.3F 37	SM 789 248
lton	.4E 41	SM 866 181
lton Cross	.5F 41	SM 877 175
lton Haven	.4D 41	SM 857 184
	.4E 41	SM 860 185
lton Haven Car Park	.4D 41	SM 859 186
rchard Beacon	.2E 73	SN 073 000
rth Beach	.2E 75	SN 133 008
rth Haven	.2D 47	SM 736 095
	.6E 47	SM 741 054
rth Pond	.2C 46	SM 723 097
of y Cae	.4D 39	SM 822 230
d Castle Head	.6E 73	SS 076 965
d School Hostel	.6C 18	SM 840 325
el y Parc Gallery & Visitor Centre	.2C 36	SM 756 252
ins Rock	.1B 46	SM 717 102
nteg	.4E 21	SM 926 348
rk & Ride Tenby, The Salterns	.2D 75	SN 128 002
e Parrog Car Park	.1A 22	SM 946 378
rsonsquarry Bay	.4F 57	SM 848 015
arson Cross	.2E 49	SM 809 099
mbroke	.4B 62	SM 983 015
mbroke Castle	.4B 62	SM 981 016
mbroke Dock	.2E 61	SM 956 037
mbroke Dock Station	.2A 62	SM 970 035
mbroke Dockyard	.2F 61	SM 962 035
mbroke Ferry	.1A 62	SM 975 046
mbroke Information Centre	.4B 62	SM 983 013
mbroke River	.3E 61	SM 952 023
mbrokeshire Coast National Park	.4E 39	SM 833 233

Pembrokeshire Coast Path		
Amroth	.4F 79	SN 172 072
St Dogmaels	.3B 8	SN 163 467
Pembroke Station	.4C 62	SM 991 011
Pembroke Upper Mill Pond Nature Reserve	.4C 62	SM 991 016
Penally	.3C 74	SS 117 991
Penally Station	.3C 74	SS 118 990
Penally Station Car Park	.3C 74	SS 118 991
Penalum	.3C 74	SS 117 991
Pen Anglas	.4A 12	SM 948 405
Penberry	.4A 30	SM 767 291
Pen Brush	.5A 10	SM 880 396
Penbwchdy	.1F 19	SM 875 372
Pen Caer	.3C 10	SM 900 414
	.4C 10	SM 908 403
Pen-Caer	.3B 10	SM 898 414
Penclegyr	.2A 30	SM 804 328
	.4A 30	SM 765 297
Pen Dal-aderyn	.4E 35	SM 715 233
Penfathach	.4A 12	SM 940 405
Penfro	.4B 62	SM 983 015
Penllechwen	.4E 29	SM 741 290
Penlledwen	.6C 28	SM 727 276
Penmaen Dewi	.6C 28	SM 720 278
Penmorfa	.4F 19	SM 872 347
Pennar	.3F 61	SM 962 024
Pennar Mouth	.2D 61	SM 942 030
Pennar Park	.3D 61	SM 947 029
Pennar Point	.2D 61	SM 944 030
Penny Bridge	.5E 61	SM 957 000
	.3D 63	SN 004 020
Penparc	.1F 9	SN 209 480
Penpleidiau	.4D 37	SM 761 237
Penrhyn	.4B 38	SM 801 235
Penrhyn Erw-goch	.6F 13	SM 991 389
Penrhyn Ffynnon-las	.4F 29	SM 750 290
Penrhyn Twll	.5D 35	SM 706 227
Penrhyn Ychen	.6E 13	SM 982 384
Pentlepoir	.2C 76	SN 116 059
Pentre-Evan Wood Car Park	.6D 17	SN 092 383
Pentre Ifan	.1D 27	SN 099 370
Pen-y-bal	.3E 15	SN 047 415
Penycwm	.4A 40	SM 850 233
Penyfeidr	.1B 40	SM 868 264
Pen-y-holt Bay	.5E 65	SR 894 954
Penyraber	.1B 22	SM 955 373
Pen yr Afr	.1C 6	SN 117 486
Picking Corner Bridge	.5C 44	SM 878 119
Pickleridge Car Park	.5E 49	SM 808 066
Pig Stone	.2B 46	SM 713 092
Pigstone Bay	.2B 46	SM 712 093
Pig y Baw	.4B 14	SM 016 402
Pill	.6D 53	SM 911 057
Pleasant Valley	.1F 77	SN 143 069
Point St John	.2E 35	SM 718 258
The Pole	.3D 65	SR 883 976
Pontbren-pwll-y-brag	.5F 17	SN 118 392
Pont Ceunant	.1E 25	SN 045 375
Pont Clegyr	.2D 37	SM 769 251
Pont Clydach	.5B 16	SN 071 390
Pont Eglwys	.5E 11	SM 924 394
Pontfaen	.4C 24	SN 021 340
Pont Fawr	.4B 20	SM 892 348
Pont Felin-wern-dew	.6C 14	SN 026 386
Pont Gelli-fawr	.4A 26	SN 062 343
Pont Newydd	.6D 15	SN 037 388
	.4B 16	SN 071 402
Pont Penarthur	.1C 36	SM 751 264
Pont Rhiw-felen	.1F 27	SN 112 373
Pont Saeson	.3F 27	SN 116 358
Pont-tre-tefa	.5F 21	SM 930 330
Pont y cerbyd	.6A 32	SM 820 272
Pont y Meddyg	.6F 13	SM 997 383
Pont y Penyd	.2C 36	SM 751 257
Pont-yr-Eilun	.6D 35	SM 708 219
Pontyr Henffordd	.3D 39	SM 827 240
Poppit Sands	.1A 8	SN 153 488
Poppit Sands Car Park	.1A 8	SN 152 485
Poppit Sands Youth Hostel	.1F 7	SN 144 488
Popton Point	.2E 59	SM 892 038
Porth Clais	.4B 36	SM 743 238
Porth Clais Car Park	.3B 36	SM 740 242
Porth Dwfn	.2A 30	SM 804 326
Porth Egr	.1E 31	SM 801 323
Portheiddy	.2E 31	SM 803 310
Porth Ffynnon	.2B 30	SM 810 328
Porthgain	.1F 31	SM 815 324
Porth-gain	.2B 30	SM 813 327
Porthgain Car Park	.2B 30	SM 814 325
Porth Glastwr	.4E 19	SM 868 342
Porth-gwyn	.5E 29	SM 747 288

Porth Lleuog	6D 29	SM 731 273
Porthlysgi Bay	4F 35	SM 729 235
Porth Maenmelyn	5A 10	SM 887 392
Porth Mawr	1F 35	SM 724 269
Porthmelgan	6C 28	SM 727 278
Porthmynawyd	5D 39	SM 826 228
Porthselau	1F 35	SM 725 261
Porthstinian	2F 35	SM 723 250
Porthsychan	4C 10	SM 906 408
Porthtaflod	4E 35	SM 716 232
Porth Tre-wen	3B 30	SM 772 302
Porth y Rhaw	3F 37	SM 783 241
Port Lion	3F 55	SM 990 085
Priest's Nose	5C 72	SS 058 971
Priory	4C 52	SM 903 072
Priory Bay	5E 75	SS 135 971
Proud Giltar	4B 74	SS 101 984
Pwll Arian	4A 10	SM 884 403
Pwll Coch	1A 16	SN 063 433
Pwllcrochan	2A 20	SM 884 364
Pwlldawnau	1F 19	SM 878 370
Pwll Deri	6A 10	SM 888 384
Pwll Deri Youth Hostel	6B 10	SM 892 387
Pwll Glas	3B 14	SN 012 411
Pwllgwaelod	5A 14	SN 003 398
Pwllgwaelod Car Park	5A 14	SN 005 398
Pwll Hir	5B 12	SM 950 396
Pwll Llong	5B 18	SM 839 332
Pwll March	5F 39	SM 842 225
Pwll Olfa	5B 18	SM 836 330
Pwllstrodur	5E 19	SM 865 338
Pwll Trefeiddan	2A 36	SM 733 251
Pwll Whiting	5C 18	SM 840 335
Pwllygranant	2D 7	SN 120 477
The Rain	3A 44	SM 857 133
Rainy Rock	4A 48	SM 763 079
Ramsey Island	4C 34	SM 697 237
Ramsey Island Nature Reserve	4C 34	SM 699 237
Ramsey Sound	3E 35	SM 713 242
Ratford Bridge	4E 45	SM 899 127
Rat Island	3F 57	SM 840 026
Red Cliff	5D 49	SM 790 066
Redstock Bridge	3E 53	SM 920 089
Renny Slip	3F 47	SM 757 087
Rhodiad-y-Brenin	6A 30	SM 767 272
Rhod Isaf	4D 35	SM 705 239
Rhod Uchaf	3D 35	SM 705 242
Rhoscrowther	3F 59	SM 904 022
Rhosycaerau	1D 21	SM 918 376
Rhyd-y-fantwn Bridge	6E 7	SN 131 438
Rhydygele	3A 40	SM 859 244
Rickeston Bridge	2E 51	SM 866 092
Rickets Head	4D 41	SM 853 189
Ridgeway	2D 77	SN 128 052
The Ridgeway	2C 72	SN 056 005
Roberston Cross	2A 52	SM 889 094
Roberston West	2A 52	SM 885 096
Roch	1F 41	SM 877 211
Roch Bridge	5C 40	SM 873 223
Roch Gate	2F 41	SM 875 209
Rosemarket	3B 54	SM 953 084
Rusheylake	3D 77	SN 129 042
Rusheylake Bridge	4E 77	SN 132 039
Rye Rocks	2D 47	SM 738 096
Saddle Head	5B 68	SR 958 928
Saddle Point	4E 69	SR 981 939
St Ann's Head	3B 56	SM 807 027
St Brides Bay	1E 43	SM 832 152
St Brides Car Park	6B 42	SM 802 108
St Brides Cross	6B 42	SM 805 108
St Brides Haven	5B 42	SM 801 110
St Catherine's Island	2E 75	SN 139 003
St David's	2C 36	SM 754 254
St Davids Bishop's Palace	2B 36	SM 749 254
St Davids Cathedral	2C 36	SM 751 254
St Davids, The Grove Car Park	2C 36	SM 756 252
St David's Head	6C 28	SM 720 278
St Davids, Merry Vale Car Park	2B 36	SM 749 253
St Davids, Quickwell Car Park	2C 36	SM 753 254
St Davids Youth Hostel	6D 29	SM 739 277
St Dogmaels	3B 8	SN 162 460
St Dogmaels Abbey	4B 8	SN 163 458
St Florence	1F 73	SN 081 011
St Govan's Car Park	4C 68	SR 966 930
St Govan's Chapel	5C 68	SR 967 929
St Govan's Head	5D 69	SR 974 926
St Ishmael's	4B 50	SM 833 073
St Justinian	2F 35	SM 724 2
St Justinian Car Park	2F 35	SM 724 2
St Margaret's Island	5C 74	SS 119 9
St Nicholas	3C 20	SM 901 3
St Nicholas's Cross	3C 20	SM 901 3
St Non's Bay	3C 36	SM 751 2
St Non's Chapel	3C 36	SM 751 2
St Petrox	3A 70	SR 971 9
St Twynnells	3D 67	SR 949 9
Sampson Cross	1C 68	SR 965 9
Sandtop Bay	6D 75	SS 129 9
Sandy Bay	5D 75	SS 128 9
Sandy Haven	4D 51	SM 859 0
Sandyhaven Pill	4D 51	SM 855 0
Sardis	3D 55	SM 970 0
	1E 77	SN 139 0
Saundersfoot	3E 77	SN 136 0
Saundersfoot Bay	3F 77	SN 144 0
Saundersfoot, Harbour Car Park	3E 77	SN 136 0
Saundersfoot Information Centre	3E 77	SN 136 0
Saundersfoot, The Regency Car Park	3E 77	SN 135 0
Saundersfoot Station	1D 77	SN 123 0
Sawdern Point	2D 59	SM 887 0
Scleddau	4A 22	SM 944 3
Scotch Bay	6C 52	SM 905 0
Scoveston Fort	5A 54	SM 944 0
Sentry Cross	4F 53	SM 935 0
The Settlands	3A 44	SM 856 1
Settling Nose	1A 44	SM 858 1
Shag Rock	3D 47	SM 737 0
Sheep Island	4F 57	SM 842 0
Simpson	4F 41	SM 882 1
Skokholm Island	6D 47	SM 734 0
Skomer Head	3B 46	SM 714 0
Skomer Island	2C 46	SM 723 0
Skomer Island National Nature Reserve	2C 46	SM 725 0
Skrinkle Haven	5F 73	SS 080 9
Skrinkle Haven Car Park	5F 73	SS 082 9
Slatemill Bridge	2A 50	SM 821 0
Sleek Stone	2A 44	SM 859 1
Sleeping Bay	5D 51	SM 855 0
Small Ord Point	6F 75	SS 149 9
Solfach	3B 38	SM 800 2
Solfach Car Park	3B 38	SM 805 2
Solfach Isaf	3B 38	SM 807 2
Solfach Uchaf	3A 38	SM 798 2
Solva	3B 38	SM 800 2
Solva Car Park	3B 38	SM 805 2
South Beach	3D 75	SS 126 9
South Haven	3D 47	SM 731 0
South Hook Point	6E 51	SM 868 0
Sprinkle Pill	1F 55	SM 997 1
Spur Island	6F 75	SS 149 9
Square and Compass	2D 33	SM 852 3
The Stack	6E 47	SM 745 0
Stackpole	1E 69	SR 983 9
Stackpole Elidor	3B 70	SR 988 9
Stackpole Head	3F 69	SR 995 9
Stackpole National Nature Reserve	3E 69	SR 981 9
Stackpole Park	2E 69	SR 984 9
Stackpole Quay	2F 69	SR 992 9
Stackpole Quay Car Park	2F 69	SR 990 9
Stackpole Warren	3E 69	SR 986 9
Stack Rock	1B 58	SM 864 0
Stack Rocks	3C 42	SM 811 1
Stack Rocks Car Park	6B 66	SR 925 9
Star Cliff	5D 75	SS 127 9
Star Rock	4D 69	SR 978 9
Stem Bridge	2C 66	SR 930 9
Stepaside	4B 78	SN 137 0
Steynton	4D 53	SM 917 0
Stop-and-Call	6F 11	SM 938 3
Strawberry Hill Car Park	4A 44	SM 851 1
Strumble Head	3B 10	SM 898 4
Strumble Head Car Park	3B 10	SM 894 4
Summerhill	4D 79	SN 152 0
Sutton	1F 45	SM 909 1
Swanlake Bay	5B 72	SS 040 9
Sychpant Car Park	3E 25	SN 045 3
Sychpant Cross	6C 16	SN 084 3
The Table	2B 46	SM 713 0
Talbenny	5E 43	SM 837 1
Teifi Marshes Nature Reserve	4D 9	SN 184 4
Tenby	2E 75	SN 132 0
Tenby Information Centre	2E 75	SN 131 0
Tenby National Park Centre	2E 75	SN 133 0
Tenby, North Beach Car Park	1E 75	SN 132 0
Tenby Park & Ride, The Salterns	2D 75	SN 128 0
Tenby Roads	1F 75	SN 140 0

...nby, South Beach Car Park	.2E **75**	SN 130 001
...nby Station	.2D **75**	SN 129 006
...orn Island	.2F **57**	SM 845 038
...orn Rock	.3E **47**	SM 740 088
...ornton	.4C **52**	SM 902 079
...klas Point	.4D **43**	SM 828 128
...rs Cross	.6F **45**	SM 906 107
...wer Point	.6A **42**	SM 788 108
...eth Llyfn	.1E **31**	SM 800 320
...cwn	.6C **22**	SM 967 326
...fasser	.6B **10**	SM 895 380
...fasser Cross	.1B **20**	SM 896 376
...fdraeth	.5F **15**	SN 057 391
...ffynnon	.5C **32**	SM 849 285
...fgarn Owen	.2B **40**	SM 868 255
...fin	.6B **18**	SM 839 325
...fwrdan	.6D **21**	SM 918 325
...eglemais	.5F **31**	SM 819 289
...groes Moor	.3F **21**	SM 939 354
...eleddyd-fawr	.6F **29**	SM 753 278
...eleidir	.5A **30**	SM 766 285
...elerw	.3E **37**	SM 773 245
...emarchog	.3C **20**	SM 901 356
...eopert	.4B **20**	SM 896 341
...etio	.5C **30**	SM 785 288
...etio Common	.5C **30**	SM 783 283
...evallen Downs	.4D **69**	SR 971 930
...evine	.6B **18**	SM 839 325
...evinert	.2D **37**	SM 767 254
...evinert Car Park	.3D **37**	SM 768 249
...ewent Point	.3F **71**	SS 021 972
...ewyddel	.5C **6**	SN 117 446
...ewyddel Car Park	.5C **6**	SN 117 446
... Maen-trai	.6A **10**	SM 880 389
...ooper's Inn	.1C **54**	SM 962 100
...wyn Bendro	.4C **34**	SM 692 236
...wyncastell	.2D **31**	SM 792 315
...wyn Cynddeiriog	.4B **36**	SM 746 239
...wyn-drain-du	.3C **34**	SM 696 249
...wyn Elen	.2B **30**	SM 819 328
...wynhwrddyn	.6D **29**	SM 730 273
...wyn Isaac	.4B **14**	SN 018 401
...wynllundain	.4C **34**	SM 692 239
...wyn Llwyd	.6B **18**	SM 832 329
...wyn-llwyd	.2F **19**	SM 878 366
...wyn Llwynog	.5D **29**	SM 732 287
	.4E **19**	SM 868 345
...wynmynachdy	.5C **34**	SM 698 226
...wyn Ogof Hen	.2D **35**	SM 708 253
...wyn-Sion-Owen	.2D **35**	SM 702 253
...wyn y Bwa	.2F **15**	SN 055 429
...dor Merchant's House, Tenby	.2E **75**	SN 135 004
...sker Rock	.2F **47**	SM 752 094
...ry Cross	.4D **77**	SN 127 032
... Canol National Nature Reserve	.1D **27**	SN 091 370
...ddewi	.2C **36**	SM 754 254
...per Hill Park	.1D **75**	SN 127 014
...per Nash	.3F **63**	SN 021 024
...per Solva	.3A **38**	SM 798 242
...chelich	.2E **37**	SM 779 254
...e Valley	.2C **76**	SN 119 053
Wallaston Cross	.4B **60**	SM 925 012
Walton West	.4B **44**	SM 862 129
Walwyn's Castle	.5C **44**	SM 873 114
Warey Haven	.5B **42**	SM 806 117
Warren	.3C **66**	SR 932 975
The Wash	.6A **66**	SR 919 942
Watch House Point	.5B **50**	SM 835 062
Waterloo	.2A **62**	SM 977 037
Waterston	.6F **53**	SM 937 057
Watwick Bay	.1C **56**	SM 818 040
Watwick Point	.1D **57**	SM 821 044
Waun Beddau	.4B **30**	SM 777 293
Waybench	.2D **47**	SM 731 099
Wdig	.6A **12**	SM 944 382
Wear Point	.1C **60**	SM 939 042
Welshman's Bay	.1A **56**	SM 796 044
The Welsh Wildlife Centre	.4D **9**	SN 188 450
The Welsh Wildlife Centre Car Park		
	.5D **9**	SN 186 449
West Angle Bay	.2F **57**	SM 847 033
West Angle Car Park	.2A **58**	SM 854 031
West Beacon Point	.6D **75**	SS 128 961
West Blockhouse Point	.2C **56**	SM 818 035
Westdale Bay	.6D **49**	SM 796 057
Westfield Pill	.5C **54**	SM 964 068
Westfield Pill Car Park	.4C **54**	SM 961 073
Westfield Pill Nature Reserve		
	.5C **54**	SM 965 066
Westhill	.5E **63**	SN 013 002
West Llanion	.2A **62**	SM 973 036
West Moor Cliff	.5A **72**	SS 033 978
West Pickard Bay	.5A **58**	SM 859 009
Whitchurch	.2A **38**	SM 799 254
Whitedole Bay	.4F **57**	SM 846 017
Whitesands Bay	.1F **35**	SM 724 269
Whitesands Car Park	.6D **29**	SM 734 271
The Wick	.3C **46**	SM 725 087
Wildgoose Race	.6B **46**	SM 711 050
Wind Bay	.4D **65**	SR 880 962
Windsor Fm	.4E **63**	SN 015 015
Winterton Marsh	.3E **49**	SM 808 087
Wiseman's Bridge	.1F **77**	SN 145 061
Wooden	.2C **76**	SN 113 055
Wooltack Point	.2F **47**	SM 755 094
Y Felin Watermill	.4B **8**	SN 165 459
Y Garn	.5D **11**	SM 915 391
Y Globa Fawr	.4D **11**	SM 916 409
Ynys Barry	.1E **31**	SM 806 320
Ynys Bery	.5D **35**	SM 702 220
Ynys Byr	.6E **75**	SS 138 965
Ynys Cantwr	.5D **35**	SM 705 224
Ynys Ddu	.6A **10**	SM 886 388
Ynys Deullyn	.4C **18**	SM 844 342
Ynys Eilun	.6D **35**	SM 707 219
Ynys-fach	.6A **18**	SM 822 327
Ynys Gwelltog	.5D **35**	SM 703 224
Ynys Meicel	.3B **10**	SM 892 412
Ynys Melyn	.6A **10**	SM 885 386
Ynys y Castell	.5D **19**	SM 851 339
Y Penrhyn	.4A **12**	SM 944 405
Y Sgwar	.2D **33**	SM 852 312
Ystafelloedd	.4A **38**	SM 791 235

Pembrokeshire Coast Path - Route Planner

St Dogmaels to Amroth

Key: 🛈 Information Centre 🅅 Visitor Centre 🛏 Hotel / B&B ▲ Youth Hostel 🍴 Restaurant 🏪 Shop
     🏕 Campsite (Seasonal opening) ☕ Cafe (Seasonal opening) 🍺 Public House 🅿 Petrol Station

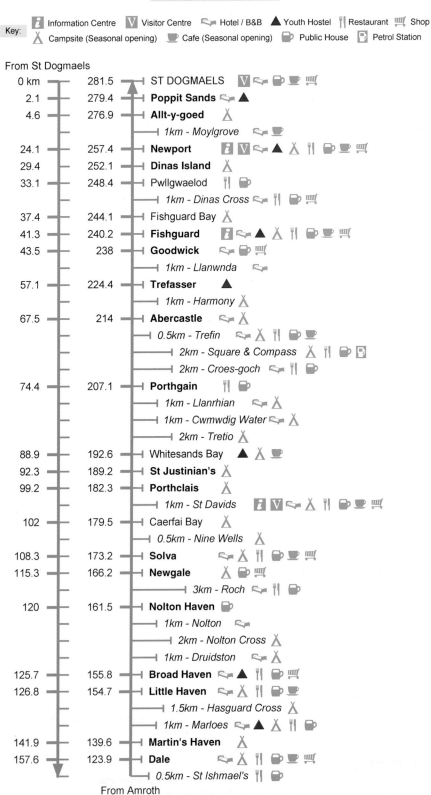

From St Dogmaels		From Amroth		Facilities
0 km	281.5	ST DOGMAELS	🅅 🛏 🍺 ☕ 🏪
2.1	279.4	**Poppit Sands**	🛏 ▲
4.6	276.9	**Allt-y-goed**	🏕
		1km - Moylgrove	🛏 ☕
24.1	257.4	**Newport**	🛈 🅅 🛏 ▲ 🏕 🍴 🍺 ☕ 🏪
29.4	252.1	**Dinas Island**	🏕
33.1	248.4	Pwllgwaelod	🍴 🍺
		1km - Dinas Cross	🍴 🍺 🏪
37.4	244.1	Fishguard Bay	🏕
41.3	240.2	**Fishguard**	🛈 🛏 ▲ 🏕 🍴 🍺 ☕ 🏪
43.5	238	**Goodwick**	🛏 🍺 🏪
		1km - Llanwnda	🛏
57.1	224.4	**Trefasser**	▲
		1km - Harmony	🏕
67.5	214	**Abercastle**	🛏 🏕
		0.5km - Trefin	🛏 🏕 🍴 🍺 ☕
		2km - Square & Compass	🏕 🍴 ☕ 🅿
		2km - Croes-goch	🛏 🍴 🍺
74.4	207.1	**Porthgain**	🍴 🍺
		1km - Llanrhian	🛏 🏕
		1km - Cwmwdig Water	🛏 🏕
		2km - Tretio	🏕
88.9	192.6	Whitesands Bay	▲ 🏕 ☕
92.3	189.2	**St Justinian's**	🏕
99.2	182.3	**Porthclais**	🏕
		1km - St Davids	🛈 🅅 🛏 🏕 🍴 🍺 ☕ 🏪
102	179.5	Caerfai Bay	🏕
		0.5km - Nine Wells	🏕
108.3	173.2	**Solva**	🛏 🏕 🍴 🍺 ☕ 🏪
115.3	166.2	**Newgale**	🏕 🍺 🏪
		3km - Roch	🛏 🍴 🍺
120	161.5	**Nolton Haven**	🍺
		1km - Nolton	🛏
		2km - Nolton Cross	🏕
		1km - Druidston	🛏 🏕
125.7	155.8	**Broad Haven**	🛏 ▲ 🍴 🍺 🏪
126.8	154.7	**Little Haven**	🛏 🏕 🍴 🍺 ☕
		1.5km - Hasguard Cross	🏕
		1km - Marloes	🛏 ▲ 🏕 🍴 🍺
141.9	139.6	**Martin's Haven**	🏕
157.6	123.9	**Dale**	🛏 🏕 🍴 🍺 ☕ 🏪
		0.5km - St Ishmael's	🍴 🍺

From Amroth

From St Dogmaels

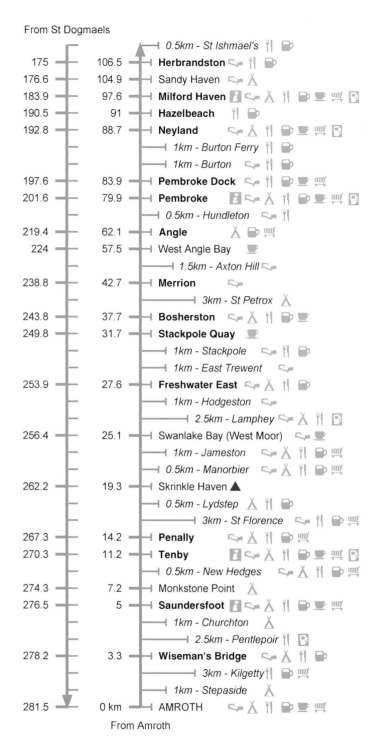

From St Dogmaels	From Amroth	Location
		0.5km - St Ishmael's
175	106.5	**Herbrandston**
176.6	104.9	Sandy Haven
183.9	97.6	**Milford Haven**
190.5	91	**Hazelbeach**
192.8	88.7	**Neyland**
		1km - Burton Ferry
		1km - Burton
197.6	83.9	**Pembroke Dock**
201.6	79.9	**Pembroke**
		0.5km - Hundleton
219.4	62.1	**Angle**
224	57.5	West Angle Bay
		1.5km - Axton Hill
238.8	42.7	**Merrion**
		3km - St Petrox
243.8	37.7	**Bosherston**
249.8	31.7	**Stackpole Quay**
		1km - Stackpole
		1km - East Trewent
253.9	27.6	**Freshwater East**
		1km - Hodgeston
		2.5km - Lamphey
256.4	25.1	Swanlake Bay (West Moor)
		1km - Jameston
		0.5km - Manorbier
262.2	19.3	Skrinkle Haven ▲
		0.5km - Lydstep
		3km - St Florence
267.3	14.2	**Penally**
270.3	11.2	**Tenby**
		0.5km - New Hedges
274.3	7.2	Monkstone Point
276.5	5	**Saundersfoot**
		1km - Churchton
		2.5km - Pentlepoir
278.2	3.3	**Wiseman's Bridge**
		3km - Kilgetty
		1km - Stepaside
281.5	0 km	AMROTH

From Amroth

- Most campsites and caravan sites are seasonal and may not be open in the winter, check before going.
- Some caravan sites are for Caravan Club members only, check before going.
- Some cafes and beach shops are only open in summer.

Backpacking

- Permission from the landowner must be obtained before camping, in any circumstance.
- Under no circumstances should a fire be lit when wild camping in the UK.

Safety & Security when walking

General

◆ Make sure you are wearing appropriate clothing and footwear, with suitable extra clothing in case the weather changes, or if you get delayed or misjudge how long it will take you to complete the walk.

◆ Be careful, if you are inexperienced, not to undertake a walk that is too ambitious.

◆ Take plenty to eat and drink, there are not always opportunities to buy extra provisions.

◆ Be sure someone knows where you are going and when to expect you back. Let them know when you have returned as well.

◆ Although taking a mobile phone is a good idea, in some remote areas there may not be a signal and therefore should not be relied upon.

◆ When walking on roads follow the advice in the Highway Code.

◆ Always use a pavement and safe crossing points whenever possible.

◆ Where there is no pavement it is better to walk on the right hand side of the road, facing oncoming traffic.

◆ Only cross railway lines at designated places and never walk along railway lines.

◆ Good navigational skills and a compass are essential.

◆ Always take warm and waterproof clothing; conditions at coastal locations can always change quickly, even in summer.

◆ Walking boots should always be worn.

◆ Gloves and headgear are advisable too in cold weather.

◆ Other essentials to take are; a waterproof backpack, "high energy" foods, a whistle, a torch (with spare batteries and bulb), a watch, a first aid kit, water purification tablets and a survival bag.

◆ Ready made first aid kits are available with all necessary items included.

◆ High factor sunscreen should be used in sunny weather, the sun can be particularly strong and can be hidden by sea breezes. Sunglasses are advisable too.

◆ Informal paths leading to beaches can be dangerous and are best avoided.

◆ When crossing a beach, make sure you know the tide times to avoid being cut off.

◆ Some cliffs overhang or are unstable and these are not always obvious.

◆ On the coast, mist, fog and high winds are more likely and can be hazardous.

The international distress signal is six blasts of a whistle repeated at one minute intervals (the reply is three) or six flashes of light at one minute intervals (again the reply is three). In an emergency dial 999 or 112.

DANGER AREA - Page 65-69. Castlemartin Range.
For further information relating to public access and live firing times contact
Castlemartin Range on 01646 662367 or visit www.access.mod.uk
DANGER AREA - Page 74-75. Penally Gallery Range.
For further information relating to public access and live firing times contact
Penally Gallery Range on 01834 845950 or visit www.access.mod.uk

The Countryside Code

◆ Be safe - plan ahead and follow any signs.
Even when going out locally, it's best to get the latest information about where and when you can go; for example, your rights to go onto some areas of open land may be restricted while work is carried out, for safety reasons or during breeding seasons. Follow advice and local signs, and be prepared for the unexpected.

◆ Leave gates and property as you find them.
Please respect the working life of the countryside, as our actions can affect people's livelihoods, our heritage, and the safety and welfare of animals and ourselves.

◆ Protect plants and animals, and take your litter home.
We have a responsibility to protect our countryside now and for future generations, so make sure you don't harm animals, birds, plants, or trees. Fires can be as devastating to wildlife and habitats as they are to people and property.

◆ Keep dogs under close control.
The countryside is a great place to exercise dogs, but it's every owner's duty to make sure their dog is not a danger or nuisance to farm animals, wildlife or other people.

◆ Consider other people.
Showing consideration and respect for other people makes the countryside a pleasant environment for everyone - at home, at work and at leisure.